Praise for *Rebels, D*

Rebels, Despots, & Saints brings together storytelling, research, and solid organizing tools in ways that connect us to the people who came before—the good, the bad, and the complicated—so that we can be the ancestors our children and grandchildren will need in order to build a more just and thriving world.

> — Innosanto Nagara, author of *A is for Activist* and *Counting on Community*

At a time when many of us feel disconnected from each other, Sandhya Rani Jha's new book reminds us that we are part of a rich and multilayered historical lineage. Using their own experiences and background, Sandhya guides us in an exploration of our own ancestors, from cultural creators to movement leaders to even the atrocious and embarrassing ones. Jha also provides engaging prompts and reflection questions to help readers apply concepts and ideas to their own lives. *Rebels, Despots, & Saints* is a necessary book for those of us seeking to better understand who we are from the vantage point of who came before us.

> — Deepa Iyer, Author of *We Too Sing America: South Asian, Muslim, Arab and Sikh Immigrants Shape Our Multiracial Future* and *Social Change Now: A Guide for Reflection and Connection*

Jha invites all ancestors to the wisdom circle to help imagine a better future for our descendants. Jha joins contemporary writers like Resmaa Menakem and adrienne maree brown and good ancestors like Baldwin and Morrison, offering readers a method for understanding their many inheritances and working in solidarity for cultural change. This is the ideal book for social change and justice groups looking to understand their place in the long struggle for freedom.

> — Patrick B. Reyes, author of *The Purpose Gap* and *Nobody Cries When We Die*

As someone who proudly claims the legacy of my ancestors, family and otherwise, I'm grateful that Sandhya Jha's *Rebels, Despots, & Saints* encourages us to not only name and retell our stories but to be mindful of the ways in which our stories are often hidden and veiled. It is in this reclaiming that we can own up to those ancestors whose stories have been misinterpreted, forgotten, or misappropriated. There are indeed rebels and despots of whom we must be proud and saints whom we must re-imagine in order to face their legacy. In every case, we must develop the strength to name and own them all. We are because of them. Read this book and clasp the ancestors to your heart once again and let them speak, but also be prepared to speak back to them as you revisit their story in your own.

— Rev. Teresa "Terri" Hord Owens, General Minister and President, Christian Church (Disciples of Christ) in the US and Canada

Rebels, Despots, & Saints is a sacred provocation and a necessary journey. A blueprint for the ages. The book prompts us to excavate fully the wisdom and life stories of those who have walked before us, and to do so with a heart intention of self-reflection and collective growth. It is a call to pull back the veil and discover the ancestral stories that may not be so apparent at first glance but that are nonetheless so important as we create pathways to healing trauma and experiencing joy. It is a divinely written text that is inclusive of quiet personal interrogation, generational acceptance, spirited enlightenment, and strong love.

— Regina Evans, artist, activist, and anti-human trafficking advocate

Sandhya Rani Jha's *Rebels, Despots, & Saints* is the book we need right now as we look for new ways to make sense of the world—and of ourselves and our histories. Warm and aware, Jha's narrative is an interesting read that helps the reader explore and understand identity and connect it to both history and spirituality. If you have a spiritual practice, seek to have one, or want to place yourself in history, this book is a must-read.

— Susan Mernit, non-profit consultant and co-founder of tech non-profit Hack the Hood and early hyperlocal news site Oakland Local

For many reasons, some of us have struggled to relate to our ancestors—blood and chosen—with meaning and reverence. Maybe like me, you've had religious training that made all ancestor connection seem like a dangerous path to worshipping dead relatives. Or also like me, when you were finally able to overcome that old religious programming, you were confused about how to connect with ancestors in the "right" ways. In this book, Sandhya Rani Jha helps us first better touch into our ancestors' stories and from there figure out how to relate to them for understanding and honestly crafting our current stories as future ancestors. If you're not sure what to think of your ancestors, not sure how to resolve your complicated histories and want to make sure you're tapping into the wise and benevolent people who made it possible for you to be here today, read *Rebels, Despots & Saints* to orient yourself toward meaningful connection across time and space.

— Micky ScottBey Jones, The Justice Doula, Enneagram teacher, facilitator, and coach

Sandhya Jha offers a nuanced and complex look at ancestors and our relationships to them. This book offers a pathway to learning and healing from our ancestors and grounding ourselves in that knowledge to become the ancestors that the next generation needs.

— Phoenix Armenta, environmental justice organizer

Rebels, Despots, & Saints offers an accessible and transformative way for humans alive today to heal from the past and move forward with purpose. Through Jha's trauma-informed approach, readers learn how to make connections between their own experiences and the collective history of oppression. This book provides a much-needed bridge between past and present, while providing a platform for sustainable action and healing justice. *Rebels, Despots, & Saints* is an essential addition to the library of anyone seriously interested in healing justice. It offers an illuminating and hopeful vision for how we can move forward together while honoring our inheritance. In short, it is a powerful invitation to take action and create meaningful change.

— Anand J.K. Kalra, Artistic & Managing Director, Uncaged Library Arts & Information

REBELS, DESPOTS & SAINTS

The Ancestors Who Free Us and the Ancestors We Need to Free

SANDHYA RANI JHA

chalice
PRESS

Print: 9780827233171

EPUB: 9780827233188

EPDF: 9780827233195

ChalicePress.com

Printed in the United States of America

To all of you, as we work together for liberation.

To Laurie Jones Neighbors, whose wisdom informed this book and who became an ancestor before we were ready for her to stop being an elder.

Contents

In order to be born, you needed:

2 parents

4 grandparents

8 great-grandparents

16 second great-grandparents

32 third great-grandparents

64 fourth great-grandparents

128 fifth great-grandparents

256 sixth great-grandparents

512 seventh great-grandparents

1,024 eighth great-grandparents

2,048 ninth great-grandparents

For you to be born today from twelve previous generations, you needed a total sum of 4,094 ancestors over the last 400 years.

Think for a moment; how many struggles? How many battles? How many difficulties? How much sadness? How much happiness? How many love stories? How many expressions of hope for the future? – did your ancestors have to undergo for you to exist in this present moment . . .

— Lyrical Zen[1]

[1]https://lyricalzen.com/ancestral-mathematics/

Introduction

The Blood in Our Veins, the Drumbeats of Our Ancestors

The great force of history comes from the fact that we carry it within us, are unconsciously controlled by it in many ways, and history is literally present in all that we do.
—James Baldwin

Roth dekha, cola becha. (See Jagannath's temple, and also sell bananas.)
—Old Bengali saying

One of my favorite youth organizations in Oakland suffered a devastating loss a few years ago. A powerful, gifted, forty-something Black man with a PhD, a head for racial justice-accomplishing public policy, and a passion for Black youth had landed at the organization just a couple of years prior. He was developing the skills to take over from the organization's founder, who had dedicated her whole adult life to community organizing and needed a break. He was helping the organization deepen its policy advocacy work. Most importantly, the Black men's empowerment group was thriving under his leadership because the youth trusted him so deeply. He had become a surrogate uncle to many of them. He then got sick with an illness we thought he would fight and win. Days turned to weeks, turned to months. He did not survive.

The funeral was packed to the walls at a large church in West Oakland, and the grief was palpable. I did not know how anyone would be able to offer comfort or encouragement. The youth no longer had their beloved leader, the one to whom they could turn and who had been committed to making them the leaders the community so needed.

1

And then one of the elders of the community began to drum. He explained the heritage and history of his drum and the style of drumming he used, which had traveled from Ghana across the Atlantic, the drumming style of the ancestors surviving the Middle Passage and surviving enslavement and surviving the New Jim Crow.

He drummed grief. He drummed solace. He drummed the solidarity and love of the ancestors into that room. In so doing, he united the youth with each other and with their ancestors, including the newest ancestor who had left them too soon but also, they were reminded, would never leave them.

This is a book about ancestors. Not ancestry per se, but ancestors: those who came before, whose wisdom we can learn from in hard times like these. There is a part of me that feels the tiniest bit guilty about writing a book that seems so internally focused at a time all of us need to be doing the work of justice in the streets.

I've been engaged in social justice work for twenty-five years, particularly in the arenas of racial justice, religious liberty, housing justice, and worker rights. For the first time in years, I'm seeing workers turn back the tide of anti-worker laws that began to become entrenched in the early 1980s with the air controllers' strike in 1981. I'm privileged to watch a resurgence of cross-racial organizing that connects racial justice issues in the US with global struggles of people who are marginalized. And I'm seeing how the next generation of justice seekers is doing a better job of creating a movement that cares for our well-being instead of burning ourselves out and using ourselves up "for the cause."

At the same time, these past few years are the first time I've had to consider what it would mean to get arrested and stay in jail, to take a punch, to have people in authority see me as part of the threat to the government they're protecting.

Other have dealt with that threat longer and more palpably. I've worked for years with people whose organizing puts their lives at risk either here or abroad because they look different than I do. I've worked with people who aren't involved in organizing and whose lives are nonetheless at risk. I work with people who have a target on their backs because of their race, gender presentation, visible sexual orientation, immigration status, or unhoused status.

But in this moment, if I care about what's happening and stand up for it, I'm at greater risk than before. Audre Lorde told us, "Your silence will not protect you."[2] I find myself aware of the fact that as voting rights are rolled back, as our policies become a greater threat to particularly trans and to all LGBTQ+ people, as the air and water become luxury commodities, and as reproductive rights are curtailed and women's bodies become battle zones for politicians, I find myself thinking that if I follow my conscience and speak out about these injustices, my relative privilege will not protect me.

Because I am also queer, mixed race, an immigrant child of immigrants, a religious leader from an interfaith family, ambivalently but realistically a person with disabilities, and gender non-conforming, I end up in relationship with a lot of younger people who don't have many mentors or elders to help them wrestle with the complex intersections of their identity.

I realize that I'm not enough. No living group of elders is enough, especially when so many of us at those intersections experienced trauma that limits what we can provide, no matter how well we want to show up. The fact that I experienced so much privilege even at those intersections is part of what allows me to stay in this work in the first place.

So, I find myself overcoming my guilt by focusing on ancestors. Because the most urgent justice work I do can't continue if I'm not—if *we're* not—paying more attention to the wisdom of our ancestors. It has become, unexpectedly, some of the least hypothetical work I do these days.

> The most urgent justice work I do can't continue if I'm not—if *we're* not— paying more attention to the wisdom of our ancestors.

Now, I know genealogy is all the rage, but that's not really what draws me to this subject of ancestors. What draws me to it is seeking the support we

---

[2]Lorde originally said in her essay "The Transformation of Silence into Language and Action," "My silences had not protected me. Your silences will not protect you." I originally came across this essay in her 1984 book *Sister Outsider* by Crossing Press although it also shows up in the posthumously published 2017 collection of essays *Your Silence Will Not Protect You* published by Silver Press.

need for this current moment in which we find ourselves, unstable and scary as it is. I think the ancestors offer us gifts to engage this moment, and we have more ancestors from whom to learn than we realize.

We sometimes assume "ancestor" means someone biologically related to us, but those aren't our only ancestors; in fact, they may not even be our most helpful ancestors. We are shaped by a lot of people who came before us, and if we pay attention to them, we may get the encouragement and inspiration we need. Our ancestors may be blood relatives, but we are also shaped by the people from our *cultural* heritage. We are who we are because of the people in our *spiritual* heritage who did brave and bold things, often in resistance to cultures of oppression around them. The people who fought for land rights or workers' rights or women's rights are our *movement* ancestors, creating the context in which we can do our work, showing us how to navigate complex political landscapes when the decks are stacked against us. While we don't often pay attention to them, the original inhabitants of the land on which we live—whom I call *landscape* ancestors—have a lot to teach us about how to be in deeper relationship with the land, with the sacred, and with each other.

I talked a little about my background already. Here's a little more. My father was a Hindu, born and raised in India (specifically the region called Bengal), and my mother is a Christian born and raised in Glasgow, Scotland. That means I have stories of ancestral strength on two continents with different histories and sometimes different ways of seeing the world. I have ancestors who survived the British, and I have ancestors who survived the Vikings. I know stories of resistance and stories of survival from both sides, from their religious texts and from the stories we prioritize.

One big thing I have learned is that there are also stories that have been hidden or suppressed because they made us look bad or weak, or they made us stand out when standing out is dangerous. There's a common saying in Hindi and Urdu: "Log kya kahenge," or "what will people say?" That fear of other people's perceptions means my family has sanitized some of their stories, left out the awkward bits, and sometimes even left out the people who stood out too much.

We change the ancestor stories in our families sometimes. We do it in our national stories, too. You and I have witnessed over the past few years a subgroup of people in our nation responding negatively, and sometimes viciously, when people of color share a robust accounting of our nation's history. Their assumption is that if we tell any of the bad, we erase all the good. The reality is that we *do* bring some of the good into question; we complicate it. This section began with a quote by the brilliant Black essayist and philosopher James Baldwin reminding us why our ancestors matter. Another quote of his is this: "What passes for history in this country is a series of myths about one's heroic ancestors."[3]

When we examine history, people from the past cease to be mythic. They turn into imperfect people. And some people don't want us to realize that all of history, good and bad, was created by imperfect people. Because that means imperfect people like us can also shape history, and that's dangerous to those who would silence us.

I'm drawn to the idea of connecting with ancestors for several reasons that aren't all that different from why I think we need to tell the whole story of our history. Most of us have ancestors whose stories have been withheld from us because their particularities somehow caused their descendants shame. But that shame says more about us and our immediate forebearers than our ancestors, and, as shame always does, it robs us of the strength we might otherwise gain from relationships with them. Indeed, we lose out on so much when those stories are concealed or altered: we miss the many resources those troublemakers, resistors, defiers-of-social convention, and the survivors of harm grant to us.

It's not just grandma's shame or dad's ambivalence that keeps us from knowing the full richness of our ancestors' lives. Sometimes we hunger so much for myths that we miss the plainer but much more valuable stories from our own narratives. For example, we may long, for very good reasons, to claim our place in families with power or position. We may fixate on a royal ancestry or embellish our connection to someone with outsized historical influence. But in addition to not being particularly true, focusing on those imagined connections may cause us to miss the rich gifts offered by our *actual* ancestors. Our serf or village-dwelling or farm-working ancestors offer us models for surviving economic oppression today; those medieval folks rose up in poor people's rebellions across the continents of Africa and Europe. We never hear those stories of their courage and thus may feel less able to challenge the unjust systems that keep us "in our place."

---

[3]Baldwin, James, "The Negro Child—His Self-Image," *The Saturday Review*, October 16, 1963.

If I were a gambler (which I'm not because legalized gambling exacerbates economic disparity), I would wager that there is always a story hidden behind our longing, our shame, our assumptions, or our aspirations. But how do we uncover what has been hidden? How do we learn to seek and listen for what lies buried beneath the layers of our society's baggage?

In 2020, I learned about Lee Anne Bell's Storytelling Project Model, which she shares in her book, *Storytelling for Social Justice: Connecting Narrative and the Arts in Antiracist Teaching*[4]. It shines a bright light on the ways the stories of our ancestors intersect and the power their stories have if we tell or even if we don't tell them. This model is an amazing resource as we work to uncover, interact with, and ultimately share our ancestors' stories. Let's start with the illustration.

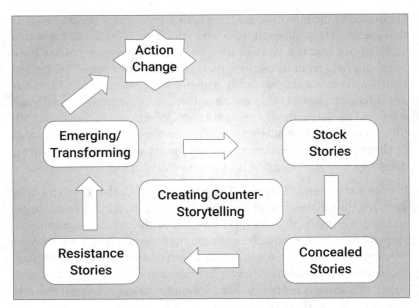

Throughout this book, we'll come back to this resource. I've used it in multiple contexts, particularly as the recurring touchstone for a series of five-week online book groups at the Oakland Peace Center during the first year of the pandemic, known as "The Beloved Book Community." In those groups, we routinely read Black/Latinx history, Afro-futurism and community organizing resources, Indigenous history, and Asian

---

[4]I am grateful to the folks at organizingengagement.org for permission to use this model. Their collection of frameworks is invaluable to serious organizers.

American memoir: writing from various voices and historical moments and social locations. In the Storytelling Project Model, we found a means of engaging all these voices with one another and with our own power to shift narratives. Working through that process not only helped us build our knowledge and understanding of our work but also allowed us to build that beloved community.

There are several desired outcomes of this exercise. First, we want to create a practice of counter-storytelling (the center box); that is, telling a fuller story than the stories that consolidate power for a handful of folks at the expense of the rest of us. In order to do that, we follow these steps:

- We notice the *stock story* that already exists in history. For example, Columbus "discovered" the Americas.

- Next, we look for the *concealed stories* that the stock story hides. Stock stories rely on erasing from the narrative the harm that was caused in the incidents they narrate. To continue the example, the stock story of Columbus conceals the brutal treatment of Indigenous people wherever Columbus went.

- We then look for *resistance stories.* If we only told the concealed stories, the stories of pain, we might trap oppressed ancestors in a simple story of victimhood, removing any agency from them and in the process taking away from us a sense of our own ability to resist. Resistance stories in this example would include the ways several Indigenous nations and many groups and event individual Indigenous people actively fought the invaders from Europe. So often, this part of our history gets skipped when it is critical for us to learn about the resistors who came before us. Learning of their presence, power, and legacy allows us to realize that we are inheritors of a narrative that may have been kept from us because it would threaten those who hold power.

- Here's my favorite move in the methodology: we look for *emerging/ transforming stories.* Those are the stories that people from the oppressed group are still engaging in today, carrying on the work of their ancestors in a modern context. The perfect example of this is the Land Back movement, where Indigenous people of many nations are demanding that the land that was stolen from them (by Columbus and so many more!), and which they consistently stewarded better than those who occupy it and govern it now, be returned. There are many ways that different groups and different nations are approaching this, but the umbrella term "Land Back" captures that diversity of strategies and the commonality of healing the land.

- After making those four moves (recognizing the stock story and whom it serves, unearthing the concealed stories of harm, looking for the resistance stories, seeking the modern-day continuation of those resistance stories as emerging/transforming stories), we use these more robust learnings to help cultivate our own work of action or change. It may be solidarity work. It may be simply sharing the more robust story with others. It may be applying those lessons to our work in a different but parallel movement. Whatever we do, we do not just sit on the information. We use it to bend the arc of the moral universe a little more toward justice.

Columbus (an atrocious ancestor if ever there was one) serves as the example here, but there is no shortage of others. I could have detailed the ways in which we celebrate the robber barons of the early twentieth century and how that stock story hides so much about the labor movement. I could have used the stock story of homesteading and land grants and what it hides about the environmental movement and about the ways the land itself resists what we do to it. (Did you know that Oklahoma has more earthquakes than California now due to fracking? That's a devastating concealed story. But what if it could become an emerging/transforming story?) I would love to use the example of how we treat British colonialism as if it were kind and polite, pinkies raised as it sipped tea, and the violence and resistance that gets erased because of that narrative.

You might be able to tell that I think this methodology is both useful and inspiring. I'm thrilled I got permission to share it with you and in each chapter. We will touch base with it to make sense of the ancestors we're hanging out with. It won't always be a linear walk through all five moves in each chapter; we might check in with them a little bit out of order. Whenever it's possible, I won't even necessarily reference the stock story. But now you'll see the methodology I'm leaning on, and I hope you'll incorporate it into your next book group, staff retreat, Q'uran study, Durga Puja family meal, or wherever you can get away with helping people shift their historic framework so that we can build justice together more effectively and build off the work of the ancestors whose stories deserve to be centered.[5]

As I've engaged with this model, here are some things I've discovered about the Rebels, Despots, and Saints who make up our ancestral trees:

- We have *romanticized ancestors*, the *stock story* protagonists in the Storytelling Project Model, the ones with power we recognize ... and who caused harm we often don't recognize.

- We have *embarrassing ancestors*, often ancestors who fit into the *resistance stories* of the SPM, the ancestors who caused trouble and got erased from the narrative because "log kya kahenge?" What will people say?

- *Overlooked ancestors* are also part of the SPM's *resistance stories*, the folks who survived or pushed back against injustice in ways we don't often enough acknowledge and celebrate. Grandma may not have been a suffragist marching in the streets and setting postal boxes on fire, but she may have taken care of the neighbor's kids while the neighbor did those things. Small contributions to the cause by people who did those small things at a big risk to themselves are important ancestors to remember.

- When I started talking about this book, I quickly realized I would have to address *atrocious ancestors*, the ones who participated in awful parts of our history. Our atrocious ancestors who turned a blind eye to atrocities or even participated in them are part of the *concealed stories* in the SPM, and it is hard for us to move forward until we've confronted them.

- Finally, there are ancestors whose stories break my heart. These are the *concealed stories* of suffering that those who came before us had to endure, stories that need to be part of our larger collective narrative.

There are so many complexities in engaging our ancestors. Who can we claim, from whom can we learn, from whom can we distance ourselves, and who can we ignore? And *who do we ignore at our peril?*

---

[5]I have actually been to several Passover seders that maybe unwittingly use the Storytelling Project Model, connecting the story of freedom from captivitiy to modern day struggles for justice and liberation.

- If we're talking about biological ancestors, we confront epigenetics, the science around *inherited trauma*, and how our ancestors' suffering codes onto us both biologically and in the ways we're taught to navigate the world around us.

- Not all of our ancestors are biological, and that is good news. If we have a sense of our culture, we have *cultural ancestors* to turn to even when we don't know our biological ancestors or if their stories of resistance have been suppressed over the years.

- In this world, we increasingly need to respond to the call of the striking coal miners from the 1930s who asked their fellow miners, "Which side are you on?" In these times, it is a real gift to know that we have *movement ancestors* to call on who can encourage us and show us how to strategize and survive what is hard now because they faced hardships also.

- Some of us feel ungrounded in this moment of so much transition. The spiritual practices of our ancestors can help ground us. The stories from sacred texts, complex as they are, might offer more stories of resistance than we realized if we read them through a lens of liberation. And sometimes our *spiritual ancestors* took on the powers that be in ways that are very relevant today.

- Those of us who aren't Indigenous sometimes live on land that we aren't in full and meaningful relationship with. The ancestors of the landscape on which we live might have wisdom for all of us, Indigenous and non-Indigenous, to learn how to reconnect with the land and each other.

Learning about our web of ancestors brings a rich tapestry of stories into all our lives. People sometimes think that is easier for me because of my diverse heritage. It's true, I am more aware of how caste, race, culture, disability, gender, class, and orientation show up in my ancestral stories. But *all* of us have a diverse tapestry of ancestors who were part of all sorts of pieces of history. In fact, that's part of why, as I wrote this book, I turned to several monthly "wisdom circles" to think through our journeys with ancestors across different lived experiences.

Once a month during 2021 I met with three groups: one of writers, one of white people, and one of people of color. I would offer prompts, share writings or reflections, or simply pose questions about our relationship to ancestors. The people who participated had so much curiosity and depth of thought on this subject. Many of them also contributed to my Patreon, so I had health insurance while I worked on the book. In addition to my cited research, most of the stories in this book come from those wisdom circles, or from conversations with friends and colleagues over many years that I did my best to recollect. (Where I misremembered details of the stories, they fixed it for me.)

It was important to me to engage white people and people of color distinctly on this subject because while our relationships to ancestors matter so much to all of us, those relationships can involve very vulnerable stories that we might not be ready to share across cultures. We might be afraid of hurting people we love, or we might be embarrassed, or we might not be ready to share our own or our ancestors' frailty across race and culture.

I was confident the people of color would enjoy hearing and sharing stories without having to filter to protect their white friends. What was exciting, though, was that in the first wisdom circle of white people, one of the participants said, "It's really important that we get a space to figure these things out without doing harm to people of color in the process." She then apologized to me for not acknowledging I was a person of color. "Well, you're doing this to help me write my book, so I think it's OK that you have the conversation in front of me," I responded fondly and a little teasingly.

Every individual's journey related to their ancestors is unique. Our experiences of culture and race contribute to those journeys for good and for ill. I'm glad I had amazing partners to think that through with. And I'm glad they were willing to let me share some of their stories with you as well. I want to be clear, though, that so much writing—on this subject and pretty much all subjects—tends to center white voices and white experiences. My goal in differentiating these voices was to create space for a diversity of voices, but I also want to clearly center those voices which have not had the microphone for most of history, in part because my experience of diverse people of color hearing each other's stories in our wisdom circle was so humbling, generous, and generative. If this whole exercise is to get beyond the stock story to the concealed story, we need to pay particular attention to, raise the volume on, those voices which have been stifled and silenced, both our own and each other's.

Another layer to the diversity of human experience I have tried to treat with care is that of both religious and non-religious readers. Some branches of the Christian family tree are deeply suspicious of the exploration of ancestors, thinking that such pursuits are somehow "pagan" or otherwise counter to a faith in Jesus. That is not my branch of the Church, obviously, and I hope readers who might be concerned would recall that throughout the Hebrew Bible *and* the New Testament, the people of God are regularly engaging with the stories of their ancestors. "My ancestor was a wandering Aramean" (Deuteronomy 26:5 NIV) is a statement of identity. Paul is constantly reminding folks that they are surrounded by "so great a cloud of witnesses" (Hebrews 12:1 KJV). This work can be an important part of growing in the Christian faith.

At the same time, though I engage a variety of religious and spiritual traditions, I want my secular social justice friends and readers here to know that these resources are for you, too; in some ways this book was intended as my love letter and letter of solidarity to and with you. You may not be interested in some aspects of this exploration of ancestors— portions may be a little "woo" for you—but I hope you'll be willing to see if there is anything here to help sustain you in what can be soul-destroying, exhausting, dangerous work. Our work is too important, the stakes are far too high, for us not to explore every resource at our disposal. As we used to say to each other at the Oakland Peace Center, "We Need Us."

In moments of exhaustion and struggle, I want you to be as assured as champion tennis player Naomi Osaka: "I would like to thank my ancestors because every time I remember their blood runs through my veins, I know I cannot lose."

. . . .

I would like to thank my ancestors because every time I remember their blood runs through my veins I know I cannot lose.
—Naomi Osaka

Our ancestors—the stories we tell, the actual historical events, the lives they lived—affect us. They shape us. So, what do we do with that reality? Some folks try to forget, thinking they have "pulled themselves up by their bootstraps." Some folks ignore the past, thinking that if they don't acknowledge it, it doesn't affect them. Some folks offer "alternative facts," like the current effort to rewrite US history books to erase things like enslavement and genocide instead of acknowledging them so we can live differently in the future.

We see the effects of not engaging what our ancestors have to teach us: white supremacy, nationalism, untreated trauma, an earth being butchered, an economy that relies on extracting our labor and leaving us exhausted so someone else can live with more resources than they know what to do with. That's a cost for all of us, people of color and white people alike.

How can we learn to look closely and see clearly, to speak the truth even when the truth implicates us, or breaks our hearts? How can we widen our circle of ancestors, to see the gifts that are being offered to us?

We can turn to ritual.

Our ancestors knew and many of us today still know that ritual is a tool to make sense of complex experiences, to honor the fullness of those experiences, and to create a container to honor what is good and healing or to heal from that which has harmed us. In fact, what draws me most to this theme of connecting with ancestors is what I've seen it offer to activists of color that strengthens us for our work of justice and helps us connect with the ancestors-in-training around us. For me, the rituals that connect us with ancestors have very concrete connections to our work in the world today. I've seen how much it empowers, encourages, and nourishes the young activists in my community. Whether you're here because you're an activist seeking some nourishment, or you've never once thought of yourself as an activist, I think that the rituals we engage really can give us strength to do our work of transforming the culture around us. Here are a few examples of what I've experienced:

- The story I shared at the beginning of this chapter, of a community of youth comforted and encouraged by a connection to their ancestors even as they grieved the loss of someone who had been their lifeline.

- At a public vigil where the voices of Black mothers were centered, in front of our city hall with its long history of police violence, the vigil started with the naming of ancestors—Black mothers who had lost sons to state-sanctioned violence throughout history, Black mothers who had resisted injustice, Black mothers who raised children who changed the world. The names reminded us of who we were accountable to, whose legacies we carried, and what was possible.

- At a spoken word performance on the theme of gentrification and displacement which was (is) ravaging the city where I live, Hmong and Latinx and Black artists shared their stories and the stories of their parents, their journeys, and their parents' journeys. The performance began with the pouring of libations, a practice to ground us in the power of the ancestors we brought into the room with us. While the tradition traces its roots back to ancient Egypt, all of us of a wide array of cultures were invited to acknowledge our ancestors as the leader poured liquid into the ground to honor those who came before.

- At the Oakland Peace Center, a collective of peace-oriented nonprofits I founded in 2012, every event and meeting begins with a land acknowledgment, where we take time to recognize that the land we gather on was originally tended by the Ohlone people who were forced off that land. We acknowledge they were forced off the land so that others could turn land into a commodity for profit, which has led to so much suffering. We also recognize that their descendants are in our midst and we commit to collaborating with them to transform our relationship with them, with each other, and with the land itself.

Sometimes our practices evoke our own ancestors. Sometimes our practices help us see and honor the ancestors of the people in the movement we love. Always, these practices push back against white supremacy, even for the people at the gatherings who identify as white, because they connect us to people navigating the world before [the construct of] whiteness was created. My hope is that, as we go on this ancestor journey together, you'll find that ritual can feed your work and nourish your soul. I believe exploring and doing this work to heal ourselves and our ancestors is so life-giving, so important to sustain us in our work but also? It is our responsibility to our descendants to work toward the world and future they deserve.

At the beginning of this introduction, you saw me include a Bengali saying: *See the temple and sell bananas*. It means set out to do one thing but manage to do two. This work of connecting with ancestors is deeply personal, but it is also a key element in how we remain better grounded, bring more of ourselves, reduce burnout and show up for each other better as people committed to building a world together. And for those of us just figuring out how to build a better world, it will give us the tools to do so. Come for your own ancestors, stay for the Beloved Community you build. Roth dekha cola becha.

One of my favorite phrases from the Movement for Black Lives came early on, maybe December of 2015, when members of the media, used to telling stories of social movements in a particular way, got really frustrated. "This is a leaderless movement!" they complained. What they meant is, "We don't know who we're supposed to interview at a given rally."

It wasn't long before the folks coordinating the Black Lives Matter rallies across the country in those early months after Michael Brown's murderer was acquitted responded to the complaint. "We're a leader-*full* movement," they said.

The youth at the beginning of this introduction, as they grieved their beloved leader's too-soon death, might have felt leaderless. But their ancestors survived and resisted and overcame so that they could be part of a leader-full movement. Their newest ancestor would be there for them as they lived into that possibility.

Almost all of us, if we can look back far enough, come from communal or "leader-full" ancestries. Our ancestors will keep showing up for us as we live into our own callings today. I hope this book will help you find out how they will show up for you.

SECTION I: The Trouble With Ancestors

In this section, we will primarily focus on the stock stories and concealed stories. What have you been told about your ancestors and why? Who is served by people believing that version of the story? Whose harm is suppressed or hidden in the telling of those stories? How do we unearth the other stories? And how do we connect with our ancestors in the process, and also as a result, of digging for the deeper story?

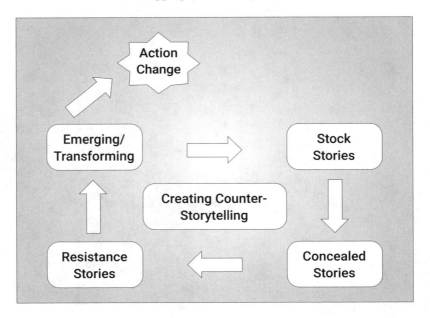

Chapter One

Romanticized Ancestors

Family secrets destroy and kill. So do historical secrets.
—*Julie Richardson*

About five years ago, I was with my buddy BK Woodson in Sacramento, California. We were part of a contingent of organizers from across the state being trained to understand how our work of racial and economic justice connected with the state's utility monopoly. I don't remember how our conversation started, but in the midst of it, I said, "I think white people actually lose something because of systemic racism; the cost of admission to whiteness is losing your culture, who you're from, your ancestors."

A Black man about ten years my senior, BK responded dryly, "I'm not convinced they've lost much." Pushing him a little, I asked, "Would you want to be white?" He evaded my question by saying, "I'd like to have all the stuff white people get." "But would you want to be white?" I persisted. He finally acknowledged that *no*, he would not want to be white. I told him I didn't know any people of color who would answer *yes*. "Because we know from whom we come," I explained. "We know whose we are."

The Storytelling Project Model encourages us to begin with an examination of stock stories, the stories we take for granted, stories that are accepted as given. Stock stories often serve to reinforce a particular view of reality. In their telling, listeners are meant to understand what is true about the world.

That definition may sound relatively benign, but my friend Cathy Myers Wirt once said to me, "When I encounter any narrative—newspaper article, poem, short fiction, story on the radio or TV—I ask one question: who benefits from me believing this story?" It's an excellent guiding question for this work.

Stock stories almost always benefit those in power, those with an interest in preserving things as they are. We grow up surrounded by them—the cultural, religious, and personal narratives that comprise our worldview. What is dangerous about these stock stories is that they are presented as "the truth, the whole truth, and nothing but the truth," while, ironically, they offer only a sliver of the truth.

In this chapter, we will look at the way certain foundational stock stories in our culture—stories about race and capitalism, and the value of human lives—have led to deep conflict, exacerbated harm, and separated us from our ancestors.

This is not to say that we do not tell stock stories about our ancestors. We do! They are likely the dominant type of stories we tell. Because stock stories offer only slivers of the truth, the ancestors we come to know through them are often romanticized versions, scrubbed of their historical context, their misdeeds and complicity, and the fullness of their humanity. When described thus, we might wonder why we bother with these stock stories at all. Though they tend to serve the interests of the few powerful folks in any community, they also grant us frameworks for understanding our lives. That can be a comfort, even if that understanding is limited. Identifying these cultural or personal stock stories in order to examine and challenge them is a critical step in coming to understand ourselves and our ancestors and equips us in the search for concealed and overlooked stories of our ancestors.

I grew up thinking it was cool that my father's family was Brahmin. That meant we were on top! If someone made a joke about dirty brown people, my father would laugh, "No! I am a good clean Brahmin!"

That stock story runs deep in my heritage. When things were hard, when we were hungry, when choices were few, when my family lived through partition in India and the ugly religious violence mixed up in it, we could always fall back on knowing we descended from the line of priests, the highest and most holy caste. A good friend of mine jokingly and ironically called herself "Tam-Brahm" because she was from the same caste, from the state of Tamil Nadu.

So, I grew up with a narrative of overromanticized ancestors intended to give me a sense of worth. It contributed to me missing my relationship with Dalit people and Indigenous people (in India called "Tribal people"), and people from disadvantaged castes. The family narrative was that we knew everyone was the same, even though my father and one cousin were the only people in generations to marry outside of our caste.

Well after I aged out of childhood, I visited a friend in Palm Springs, California. I took a beautiful, less traveled road through desert and arid hills. As the road wound across the wide expanse of brown terrain, I would occasionally come across small collections of RVs and trailers in informal encampments. That wasn't unusual—mobile living has increased across the country as life gets harder for people who aren't in the top ten percent of wealth. What was unusual, though, was that most of the encampments had three types of flags flying from various campers and trailers and RVs—the US flag, the Confederate flag, and most frequently the "Don't Tread on Me" flag, otherwise called the Gadsen flag after the soldier, slave owner, and South Carolina politician who is credited with creating it during the American Revolution. That flag became increasingly politicized over the years, adopted by groups who repurposed it to stand for white supremacist purposes. (That said, most of us don't know that the flag originated from someone who didn't want to be trodden on, but who felt entitled to tread on other human beings by enslaving them.)

I find myself pondering that tangling of a revolutionary war flag with a flag of secession, and I wonder how much that has to do with the ways we're all encouraged to overromanticize some of our nation's history. When I was in second grade in Akron, Ohio, the same year I became a US citizen, well into Ronald Reagan's second term in the White House, our music teacher wrote a medley of songs about the US for our class to perform. We sang a line from the *Pennsylvania Polka*, a line from *Take Me Home, Country Roads*, a line from the Ohio fight song, and right there in the middle, right there in northeast Ohio, we sang:

I wish I was in the land of cotton, old times there are not forgotten,
Look away, look away, look away, Dixieland.
I wish I was in Dixie, hooray, hooray!
In Dixieland I'll take my stand to live and die in Dixie.

—Dan Emmett, *Dixie* (1859)

There's a stock story surrounding the US Civil War that *Dixie* is about culture, not racism. That story hides several concealed stories of before, during, and after the war: the ongoing and institutionalized dehumanization of Black people on both sides of the Mason Dixon line, the exploitation of poor white people in the South (as well as in the North), and the campaign of violence against Indigenous people and continued theft of their land.

We're in an economically precarious time right now, and in unstable times it is not surprising that people turn to stories that help them feel grounded in their dignity and worth at a time they do not feel valued in the world as it is now. We can turn to ancestors who say, "we used to have power; we deserve power." In the process, we might have to turn a blind eye to the wrongdoings of those ancestors to support our narratives. (The reality is, very few people with the power of royalty held onto that power without doing some horrible things. It's the same as how people have begun to name that you can't to be a billionaire today without exploiting workers or manipulating customers or some other fashion of doing harm.)

Henry Louis Gates's show, *Finding Your Roots,* features prominent figures learning about their ancestral origins. It always makes for good television as actors and public figures we know learn things about their heritage they had never known before. Some of their discoveries are beautiful— Queen Latifah discovering the rich story of the powerful Black woman after whom she was named. Some of the discoveries are heartbreaking— Don Cheadle learning that his ancestors remained enslaved for years after emancipation because their enslavers were Navajo, who, as part of a sovereign nation, did not have to end enslavement when the United States did but banned it several years later. Part of why the show is captivating is the reminder that if these celebrities' ancestry is so complex, ours might be as well.

In 2020, Gates was interviewed about the import of that show in that moment and its contributions to the nation's zeitgeist. Gates talked about how for many Americans, there had, for decades, appeared to be an arc of life improving, each generation doing a little better than the one before, with greater access to basic human rights than the generation before, and so forth. In an interview almost exactly a year before the storming of the US capitol, he then noted a shift in that trend. To me, the quote captures everything about what it can mean to examine overlooked ancestors instead of desperately clinging to overromanticized ones.

> Now there are many Americans, I would say the majority, who can't assume that curve of progress. And so, people are unsettled. Traditional foundations that provided stability have been rocked. It used to be the church. It used to be economic progress. It used to be that people believed in the Constitution and respected it and the Declaration of Independence. Now all these things are, if not under erasure, at least questioned. So, people are looking for other forms of stability. And one form that they found is right under your own feet, which is the roots that you stand on, the ancestors on whose shoulders you stand. One way to address your own erasure is to un-erase your ancestors, to establish their identity, to know where you come from.[6]

Many of us can still see the images from when a collective of right-wing extremists stormed the capitol building while Congress was formalizing the 2020 election results. I picture the same combination of flags I saw scattered across the informal RV camps in the desert of southern California: US flags, "Don't Tread On Me" flags, and Confederacy flags. Flags that, in the hands of people seeking to undermine democracy, represented overromanticized ancestors.

Stock stories not only do a disservice to some but also to those we might assume would benefit from them. My father described one occasion in his early life in which he began to catch a glimpse of the harm and irrationality of his own internalized privilege as a Brahmin. On this particular day, he had to walk ten miles from the train station to his village in the muggy heat of a Bengali summer. He was weak with thirst by the time he came across a woman pulling water from a well, about halfway to his village. He asked her to pour some water into his hands,

---

[6]Henry Louis Gates, interview on Amanpour & Co., 01.16.20

but just before she did, he paused and asked, "Are you Brahmin?" She said "No, I'm Muslim."

Brahmins were prohibited from accepting water from people from the "wrong" caste or from outside of their caste system, so hearing her answer, he shook his hands and walked away thirsty. He was so thirsty in fact that a little way down the road, he knelt on the ground and scooped up some water from a stagnant puddle.

Now, my father obviously suffered physically from thirst because he chose in that moment to honor a set of arbitrary rules about who was considered clean. He suffered for upholding that stock story of the higher worth of Brahmins than others. But he also told me that story to help me see that the episode was just the tip of the iceberg. A woman who is not even allowed to offer water to a neighbor because of her religion will certainly not have the agency to navigate systems of power that might grant her access to things like an education. Those systems, which exist to reinforce those power differentials, are remarkably effective. A Muslim woman at the time would not have been able to pursue the kind of education my father did. Without that education she could not leave the village as he was able to, an opportunity which led to his far more prosperous life.

The same systems that left him thirsty for a morning (and at no small risk of cholera!) nevertheless provided him, and later me, with almost embarrassing access to opportunity. Those systems continue concentrating access and control over generations, in ways that absolutely continue to harm the people in our 80 percent Muslim village to this day. (No one from my family lives there anymore. We have all had the chance at a different life and took it.)

The thing I so appreciate about my father's retelling of this story is that while he named how the stock story harms him, he always understood that the harm was greater for the woman. I have found that this is one of the hardest things for people to navigate as we examine our romanticized ancestors and our own privilege: how some people can both benefit from and be harmed by a system, and how to make sense of the disproportionate harm done to some and not others. This difficulty simmers beneath the surface of the Confederate flag waving Californians, and even in white people who are trying to do the work of expanding justice.

As I talked with my friend BK about whether he'd rather be Black or white, he looked at me with increasing skepticism. We stood quietly, a little tensely, for a few seconds before I assured him that it was not his job to worry about what white people lost because of racism.

That conversation got me thinking about the anger some white people exhibit when they are reminded that people of color are connected to a culture. It is not necessarily the *fault* of any given contemporary white person that their ancestral history and culture in the United States has become synonymous with, for example, capitalism and white supremacy. Generations before them were taught that if they wanted to get ahead, they should drop whatever vestiges of their ethnic particularity remained and jump on into the melting pot. The traditions and cuisine, the clothing and music, the ancestors, and the community ethos, were all sacrificed to something that was meant to be particularly "American." Something that, of course, excluded anyone who wasn't white (or Christian). This loss may not be entirely understood by white Americans today, but it is surely felt. And, for no small number, it is felt as anger. People of color, like me, are antagonized and marginalized and punished for that loss and by that anger.

Speaking with BK got me thinking about an anti-racism team I was part of almost twenty years prior. I had missed a session where we were being trained, and a friend who led it complained about how badly behaved some of the leaders had been, even though it was their second time going through the training. There was an exercise (very much of its time) about halfway through the four-day training where the Asian Americans got together, and the Black attendees, and Indigenous, and Latine, and white. Each group was tasked with writing a list of things they loved about being from that race. Black people often wrote about food, laughter, resilience, brilliance, and stories. Asian Americans also wrote about food, family, work ethic, and tenacity in the face of hardship. By that point in the training, white people had learned whiteness was a construct, and most of them had had their cultural heritage stripped away from them in exchange for access to resources at the expense of people of color. So generally, white people's lists included "I am grateful that I do not get followed around department stores when I am shopping" and other things that acknowledged privilege.

At this training, however, some of the white leaders seemed to have grown tired of having to talk about white privilege, so they wrote down things like "bagpipe music." Afterward, when my friend debriefed with me, she recounted this surprising bit of cultural pride. "Like any of them ever listen to bagpipe music!" she yelled in frustration. "Maybe if they did, they'd stop being angry at us for having our culture," I replied tentatively. She, like BK twenty years later, was not compelled by my argument. Her frustration lay, understandably, with the fact that they had written down "bagpipe music" to avoid dealing with the uncomfortable issue of white privilege. That discomfort showed up (and shows up) in pretty much every training because white privilege is an uncomfortable thing to acknowledge, even knowing it's not the fault or choice of the white people attending the training. My colleagues who comprised the group of trainees were not engaged in an authentic effort to connect with their cultural heritage; they were trying to deny that they had been racialized.

I mentioned before the ways in which I'm called to be an elder (although I'm fairly young for that role) because my trauma has been mitigated by my privilege in ways different from many other queer people of color. I keep learning how to recognize both the trauma and the privilege so I can keep showing up well for people who do not have as many elders as they deserve and need. I do so humbly because many queer and trans people of color in the generation above mine and even of my own generation did not have the privilege of getting old enough to become elders themselves.

Because of the complex intersections of privilege and trauma, it is all the more important that we do the work of critically engaging the stock stories that shape us and those around us. We can also interrogate why we are motivated to seek out certain types of ancestors.

My friend Lia caught the double-edged sword of romanticizing and overlooking all in a couple of sentences when she reflected with the white people's wisdom circle I facilitated in 2021, "You might even call some types of ancestors 'trendy.' My grandmother used to say that she counted our ancestors all the way back to Mary Queen of Scots. My other side of the family always says that one of my grandmothers was 100 percent Cherokee, which is also another conversation about how Indigenous people were both revered and hated."

This reminded me of a heartbreaking story my friend Rachel told me about spending time with her grandmother with dementia in Texas.

Rachel said her grandmother had encouraged her to take pride in her Cherokee heritage as well. "But sometimes her dementia actually caused her to share parts of our story that she protected and covered up when she was what the doctors would call 'lucid,'" I remember Rachel saying. So one day, Rachel asked her grandmother who had taught her how to make such good pozole. In earlier years, her grandmother had always said the family had a Mexican cook. Today she said, "I learned it from my mother." (Her mother, who was supposed to be Cherokee.) "Not from your cook?" Rachel clarified. "No," her grandmother assured her. "From my mother." When Rachel visited her on a "better memory" day and followed up, the story had gone back to the one Rachel had grown up hearing. Rachel was inclined to believe the newer story because she, too, has learned to look for where the dominant culture was served by a particular stock story and who benefits from telling the story that way.

If non-Indigenous people believe Indigenous people are a romantic historic artifact, there's a little shine they get from connecting to that legacy. But while most Mexican people are of Indigenous heritage, Mexicans in the US, Mexican Americans, and Chicanos are very much present and also stigmatized. That association does not preserve power for a family seeking to be included in and protected by the dominant narrative's stock story.

It is also worth noting that this reverence for Indigenous ancestry only works because the other stock story is that Indigenous people were noble and wise *and that they no longer exist.* Real-live Indigenous people are rendered invisible and ignored to preserve a romanticized stock story that serves the status quo.

Rachel holds onto that story not to claim a cultural experience she wasn't shaped by but to remember why she stays committed to anti-oppression work: so that everyone is allowed to and wants to tell their full stories.

It's not just the power and prestige of royalty or the cliché of being a white person with Indigenous heritage; there are other ways folks lay claim to the stock stories of our varied cultures. Some of my friends from Latin America have told me that not so long ago, people liked to brag about their Castilian roots as if being part Spanish made them superior to people with more Indigenous blood. So, too, when I was a young adult in the late nineties and early 2000s, I got to hear many Black activists tell Black children to remember that they were descended from kings and queens in Africa, no matter how much this country tried to deny their dignity and worth.

In some ways, some of those narratives have receded, perhaps because we have increasingly complex narratives about people in positions of authority. The romance is fading. But let's more closely examine how those stock stories arose, and the ways they continue to influence us.

The power of colonizers isn't only their military might. It is their ability to keep telling the story of how they won because they are superior, generation after generation, until the people they are oppressing come to believe it despite themselves. That means the power of colonizers can last for generations after they have left. As a result, Castilian blood was seen as a sign of relative superiority, relative civilization, and a certain level of regalness, maybe.

At the same time, some children cannot trace their biological lineage to before their ancestors were forced to these shores and enslaved. Additionally, this horrific injustice forced on their ancestors is used to say that they are in some way inferior, which is how race-based enslavement was justified in the first place. This counter-narrative, that they are descendants of kings and queens, reminds children that they come from origins of greatness and to carry themselves with pride.

Some of those narratives are thinning out as people recognize the conquistadors and the royals aren't always the good guys. I also know we have a longing to have worth, to come from worth, which lets us sometimes cling to unhealthy narratives.[7]

Many of these narratives are tied up in what I might call (after the wisdom of my friend Claire) the triumvirate of oppression—capitalism, racism, and ableism. These three forms of systemic oppression are inextricable from each other but are often discussed individually (if

---

[7]During Black History Month 2019, 6th grade teacher Bradshaw decorated her classroom door with these words from the Rev. Nadine Drayton-Keene: "Dear Students, they didn't steal slaves. They stole scientists, doctors, architects, teachers, entrepreneurs, astronomers, fathers, mothers, sons, daughters, etc., and made them slaves. Sincerely, your ancestors." This re-framing of powerful ancestor stories offers a powerful model for claiming overlooked ancestors as we seek wisdom from those who came before. https://people.com/human-interest/jovan-bradshaw-slavery-lesson-door-black-history-month/

discussed at all).[8] So much of how we understand or articulate what it means to be human relates to the establishment of a global extraction economy[9] (which you might refer to as capitalism), white supremacy or racism, and ableism. The stock stories we tell about what kinds of lives have the most value stress an able-bodied white person's ability to make money. And many of us, subconsciously or otherwise, measure both ourselves and our ancestors against those values.

The Oakland Peace Center, the not-for-profit organization I founded and ran for ten years, got to co-host a video series on capitalism back in 2018 that our friends at East Point Peace Academy organized, because if we were seeking to establish Beloved Community, we needed to better understand the root causes of Beloved Community's antithesis. I learned so much from that series, including the many ways Adam Smith shaped our dangerous and violent narrative around capitalism by pretending that it wasn't founded on enslavement, genocide, and the exploitation of poor workers in a transnational economy. His book that is still used to frame capitalism today, *Wealth of Nations*, written in 1776 (in Scotland, much to my chagrin), reads as if monetary exchanges happen in a fair and generally local community where competition happens among bakers across the road from each other rather than between lords with generational wealth who have access to fully staffed ships on the one hand and a local baker on the other.

The way the British government practiced this form of "fair competition" in relationship to their colonies is painfully illustrated in their response to the Great Potato Famine that plagued Europe in the 1860s, including Ireland, as described in an article by the History Channel.

---

[8]In fact, we're getting very much outside my arena of expertise in this section. My colleague BK Woodson and I named the three sins of this land "patriarchy, exploitation of land (genocide) and exploitation of labor (particularly enslavement)," and talked about racial capitalism in conversation with sexism. When Claire suggested this different trio, I knew it was a stretch for me, but also it resonated so deeply: how for generations we had been told we were only valuable for what we produced, which devalues anyone who is not "producing" that which serves capitalism. Eugenics and death camps and the medical profession all engage ableism and capitalism and racism in ways that would require a new book. So, thanks for exploring this new-to-me framework with me.

[9]I learned the term "extraction economy" from my colleagues at Movement Generation and find it a much more specific term that gets at what I actually want to fix. Capitalism feels nebulous and unclear to me, but I know what an extraction economy is and what the alternatives to it are. For a great intro to this framework, check out this video: https://www.youtube.com/watch?v=eIzV_r398dU

British lawmakers were such adherents to laissez-faire capitalism that they were reluctant to provide government aid, lest it interfere with the natural course of free markets to solve the humanitarian crisis. "Great Britain cannot continue to throw her hard-won millions into the bottomless pit of Celtic pauperism," sneered the Illustrated London News in March 1849. Charles E. Trevelyan, the British civil servant in charge of the apathetic relief efforts, even viewed the famine as a divine solution to Hibernian overpopulation as he declared, "The judgement of God sent the calamity to teach the Irish a lesson, that calamity must not be too much mitigated."[10]

Notice how a stock story about fair competition in the open marketplace emerges in ways that will devastate generations of poor people, people of color, women, and more. Take a few moments to pause and think of all the ancestors harmed by this stock story.

While enslavement had been in existence in various forms for many years, this was also the period that race began to become a pseudo-science to justify the enslavement of and genocide of and economic exploitation of certain groups of people.[11] In fact, the categories would continue to evolve for hundreds of years in order to serve the people with the most wealth. So, the creation of race to prop up an economy grounded in exploitation is the foundation of that economic system, which is why many people call it "racial capitalism." Yet another stock story had been created about the heroic strength of European adventurers and the inferiority of the people they encountered, killed, conscripted or enslaved. Pause again and think of your ancestors who suffered needlessly because of this stock story. They deserve your grief.

Ableism shows up so enmeshed with capitalism that some of us don't even notice it operating. The stock story is a powerful one, but it is a

---

[10]https://www.history.com/news/when-america-despised-the-irish-the-19th-centurys-refugee-crisis

[11]If the term "racial capitalism" is a new term to you, my friend Claire pointed out this excellent video that shows how "capitalism requires inequality and racism enshrines it." https://antipodeonline.org/geographies-of-racial-capitalism/ While I've noted that capitalism was developed in ways that also exploit poor white people, Claire makes the equally important point that colonization and race are *always* embedded in modern capitalism.

stock story, not a universal story. The stock story of capitalism could not function without creating a narrative about people having value based on their contributions to capitalism. The tragic impacts of this stock story showed up multiple times in how public policy and public health strategies sought to address COVID, almost always treating people with significant risk factors as disposable.

I remember one time someone in a group session for my training as a minister asked, "Can you let us love you without you having done something to earn it?" While I knew he was trying to help me have some sort of spiritual breakthrough, I remember laughing and saying *no*, I actually couldn't. My sense of my own value was thoroughly wrapped up in my need to be productive, and I was trained in it well by generations who had to work hard to survive and to support their families and had come to equate it with morality instead of exploitation in a world that did not actually need them to work that hard in order to thrive.

Many of us come from cultures that had ways of honoring elders. Some of us come from cultures that saw disabilities as a sign of being touched by the gods. Some of us come from cultures where people with intellectual disabilities were seen as having vision. Capitalism took away from all of our ancestors the possibility of a culture that honored people for who they were instead of what they contributed materially to that extraction economy. Modern-day capitalism took away the value of *being* and replaced it with the value of *doing*. That not only misshapes our relationship to our ancestors, whose value has been forced through the lens of productivity; it also misshapes our understanding of what our own value is because that ancestral wisdom has been lost. And for ancestors who lived through more recent times, particularly since the development of the bell curve that created an imaginary "norm" that has been used in many violent ways, we have ancestors whose lives were made miserable not because of their disabilities but because of ableism. We have ancestors who were tortured in an attempt to "fix" them instead of fixing the violent stock story. We have ancestors we may never have learned about because they could not contribute to capitalism and were therefore deemed unworthy of remembering.

So much of the grief we carry for ancestors stems from the enmeshment of those three oppressions, those violent stock stories, the unholy trinity of capitalism, racism, and ableism. That includes the ancestors whose stories have been withheld from us for many reasons: queer and trans ancestors, ancestors of different gender expressions, ancestors with disabilities, and ancestors who did not fit into the stock stories that shape our world.

For white people, it is also wrapped up in the ancestors who were taken from them because their assimilation into this constructed identity came at the cost of knowing those ancestors. That also deserves grief.

My colleague and now ancestor, Laurie Jones Neighbors, brilliantly underscored this point in an essay she wrote about the book *Indigenous Prosperity and American Conquest: Indian Women of the Ohio River Valley, 1690-1792* by Susan Sleeper-Smith. Neighbors explained that Smith opens the debate over whether Tecumseh "should be credited with the strong pan-tribal movement of this time period." Instead, Smith says, "the influence and relationships necessary to that alliance can be attributed to Ohio Indian women [who had] for centuries been working together to harvest riparian, wetland, and terrestrial resources on a truly grand scale and to build a thriving peltry export economy." Neighbors continued:

> European visitors were flabbergasted by the "modernity" of Wabash Indian villages and bustling trade centers like Miamitown, where Indians from many tribes, French and British traders, and blended Indian and French families lived in sturdy homes, developed their own style of high fashion from Indian tradition, European cloth, and Montreal silver, and basically had a sweet life for a very long time.

> This woman-led, cooperative society and nascent urbanity was all but erased by Kentucky settlers and American politicians, and with it, Indigenous women of the Ohio River Valley have been backgrounded by a long line of male historians who have allowed themselves to be organized by the logic of patriarchy, capitalism, and colonialism, replacing hardworking, innovative Indian women with the likes of the Johnny Appleseed myth. How could Indians of the American trope be Indians if they drank tea from French china?[12]

---

[12]https://citiesandpeople.com/ljnc-blog/2019/6/19/1100-silver-brooches-and-a-tool-for-thinking-about-transformative-change

In other words, the erasure of Indigenous ancestors' full stories prior to westward expansion serves the stock story, and the creation of that stock story requires brutal acts of violence, eviction, forced marches, and murder in order to thrive.

There are many reasons we have been raised with stories of romanticized ancestors. More often than not, those stories have been handed down to give us a sense of dignity and worth in a world that extracts all it can from us and in some instances tells us how little value we have. Simultaneously, though, those romanticized ancestors prop up narratives that keep things the way they are. The best of our ancestors wouldn't love the way things are. So the work of challenging those stock stories of our powerful, royal, or extinct ancestors is part of the work of getting to know our ancestors in more meaningful, more empowering, and more justice-shaping ways.

Where We Can Go From Here

○ *If you want to write and reflect on this chapter's theme in your own life:*

Take some time to consider the stories you got about the people who came before you. Reflect on whether they aligned well with our dominant culture's values around money, around success, around family structures. Why were those the stories you heard? What other stories do you want to know about?

○ *If you want to engage a personal ritual around this chapter's theme:*

If you have a photo of a relative who has passed away who did a lot to preserve the stock story, take out that photo. Look at that person and tell them what you've learned about how the world is different than how they understood it. Take some time to sit with the truths you've named. Imagine how they might respond differently now than when they were alive.

○ *If you want to engage your activist or spiritual group in a practice*
   that will help them begin to connect with ancestors in new ways as
   part of their work to dismantle white supremacy:

   Share with others what stock stories exist in your family stories.
   Invite your colleagues to imagine how they would engage one
   of your romanticized ancestors compassionately but clearly
   about what they created that we have to undo now. Name how
   you will move beyond your ancestors' stock stories.

   Even those of us who have experienced marginalization have
   some stock stories in our families' ancestor stories—stock
   stories that prioritize the well-being of people based on sex,
   gender, class status, immigration status, etc. Sometimes those
   things are hard to see but are usually there.

Chapter Two

Embarrassing and Overlooked Ancestors

There is beauty in our roots. Sometimes we think our roots are shameful, and people tell you that you're no good or your ancestors are no good or that you come from a neighborhood of no hope and terrible crime. But it's about the beauty of those places, and I carry that with me.

—*Luis Alberto Urrea*

My third cousin, Cissy, back in the 1920s, decided to research our family history. Genealogy was all the rage in those days. Everyone was finding out how they were connected to some ancient duke or earl or queen. Cissy wanted to know our family's royal heritage as well. Genealogy websites weren't a thing (any websites were a few generations from being developed), so she asked Granny Caldwell to help her fill in the family tree. She had found a name whose lineage she hadn't been able to trace. How far back, she wondered, could Granny Caldwell trace our ancestry in the McMillan line?

"The only McMillan I know," Granny Caldwell ruminated, "is ol' Jack O'Mullen, the tattie howker." Thus ended Cousin Cissy's career as a genealogist. "The moral of the story," my mother explained many years later, "is some people forget they were born up a close." If you're lost, here's a little bit of translation:

- O'Mullen is an Irish name (not a Scottish name).

- A tattie howker is a potato picker, usually a migrant farm worker from West Ireland hired by Scottish merchants as seasonal labor (not what you'd call a royal or noble profession).

- A close is the narrow entryway of a tenement building where poor people are crammed into tight quarters.

Cousin Cissy wanted a noble story to brag about, and instead, she was given a narrative of people she wouldn't have been all that proud to have descended from or, at the very least, wouldn't have been bragging about. Can't put on airs about an Irish tattie howker. *The very reason* Granny Caldwell told her that story was to remind her where she came from and not to think too highly of herself. We honestly have no reason to believe Granny Caldwell didn't make up Jack O'Mullen just for shock value.

One of the things I love most about this family story is that it gets told in the first place. Cissy was in hot pursuit of a romanticized stock story and Granny Caldwell offered her a tattie howker. Jack O'Mullen's ordinary laborer status (or, worse, *Irish* laborer status!) isn't hidden away at all. That is so often not the case in family stories. It happens so frequently that a critical part of the Storytelling Project Model is interrogating the stock stories of strong leaders and great victories until we're able to uncover the hidden, or concealed stories of our ancestors—the stories of how our ancestors were harmed by people with power. Beyond that, the SPM is helping us dig deeper for the *resistance stories.* These are the stories of those who challenged the status quo, who showed insufficient commitment to keeping up appearances.

Our embarrassing and overlooked ancestors are more likely to be poor, female, and to remind us of parts of our heritage that the dominant culture looks down upon. Their stories hold a complexity that our stock stories cannot hold. Instead of racial purity and clear lineages to royalty, many of us have actual ancestors who defy easy categorization, whose lives have hidden or lost narrative threads.

Stock stories are reinforced in multiple ways, and our embarrassing and overlooked ancestors (and peers) are silenced by forces even beyond our families' reach. During the Trump administration and its aftermath, for example, many political pundits sought to understand "working class America." But those pundits weren't generally talking about, or concerned with, women of any race or people of color of any gender, even though women and people of color make up a significant portion of the working class. What pundits meant was "white men experiencing work insecurity in under-resourced, predominantly white communities." What they said was "working class."

Moving beyond the stock story enables us to uncover the horrors and suffering that are often ignored. Once we hear those previously muffled voices, our ears grow increasingly attuned to resistance stories: those that remind us that oppressed people are more than just victims.

Emerging stories help us connect modern-day justice movements to their legacy rather than act like modern-day struggles come out of nowhere, which helps us remember the historic injustices we can all resist.

In two separate wisdom circles that contributed to this book, participants shared stories of embarrassing and overlooked ancestors. Sara, a white woman, told our group a powerful, riveting, and nevertheless hidden story of her family ancestors, one that I would have thought anyone would be proud to claim. In doing some research, she learned that her great-great-great-great grandfather was "killed by Confederate rebels during the Civil War." She and her siblings tried to find further details to no avail and expressed shock that their grandfather hadn't told them that story, a story of an ancestor on southern soil who resisted the confederacy in such a way that they killed him for it. They assumed, given the dramatic and righteous nature of their ancestor's death, that their grandfather must not have known at all.

As they shared their findings with the rest of the family, Sara's father said, "I remember that story. I've read a newspaper article about it. The killers made his mom fix them breakfast." Sara's father had been the generation to let that story die.[13] But why?

Vanessa, in the circle for people of color, talked about her aunty and how the family didn't talk about her much except as a cautionary tale.

---

[13]The family story Sara was eventually able to unearth is profound and moving, and I hope that if Sara finds it helpful, she'll share the story at some point. For now, though, know that it was a story worthy of being honored in family memory as both painful and powerful.

Vanessa shared that this aunt didn't follow a lot of convention about how to behave in the community where they lived. One of the things Vanessa's aunt did that was unusual, and caused her family no small amount of social discomfort, was keeping alive the Indigenous Filipino traditions around healing plants and herbs. As Vanessa connects with those same ancient practices of ancestral medicine years later, she has come to realize what a loss it is that the family discouraged her from learning from the wisdom of an ancestor, and that they did so specifically because she stood out in ways that made them uncomfortable. But Vanessa and I can't help but wonder why they were uncomfortable to begin with.

· · · · · · · · · · · · · · · · · · · ·

What stories do you only have pieces of because your family didn't want to claim those stories too much? Why do you think they didn't love those stories?

While a lot of this book will focus on how race, as it is practiced in the United States, has shaped our ancestral stories, the intersectionality of class will also be evident at times. The reality is that some of us have been given stories that glorify our humble roots, sometimes as a means of distancing us from the forms of privilege from which we benefit now. Common versions of this are, "we can't be racist; we grew up without two nickels to rub together," or "don't tell me we're privileged; when we came to this country your father and I each had only two outfits, one to wear and one to wash."

However, for many of us, stories have been withheld from us about our ancestors because they disrupt the longed-for state of *normalcy* that is part of the American narrative, particularly the middle-class American narrative. Obviously, "normal" is a subjective term, a myth made up for a million reasons, and yet "normal" shows up to disrupt access to the stories of our ancestors in families seeking safety in what it means to be part of the middle class. Even as people whose incomes put them in the middle class dwindle by the day, we are trained to long for the "normalcy" of that class status.

It is impossible to say for sure, but as Sara explored her family's story, she wondered if part of why her father hadn't thought to share the story was this: his generation had a utilitarian relationship with family history. Anything that didn't have visible use could be disposed of. As she discussed the story with the group, we also wondered together if some of it had to do with her family having moved to a community where not sticking out was upheld as a value, so that even a story where her ancestors were admirable wasn't a story worth preserving, because it made the family unusual.

Similarly, as Vanessa shared the story of her aunt in a different group, we reflected on the things colonization had taught us. Ancestral wisdom became dangerous because it was unchristian according to missionaries. Behaving in ways that deviated from the norm created by the missionaries was also unchristian. Being faithful and being "normal" became intertwined in ways that choked out Indigenous cultural expression in favor of replicating the culture imposed by missionaries. Over generations, that connection between faith and cultural behaviors was internalized by people living in the missionized community, so that the stories of culture keepers became dangerous stories, upsetting the stock story and endangering the missionized status quo.

What class does your family consider itself? Do you see ways in which your class shapes the kinds of stories you have learned or that you tell about family who came before? How do those stories adhere to or challenge assumptions about your experience of class?

Folks who work to end classism name four or sometimes five classes in US society which have to do with socioeconomics and with other cultural markers. The classes are wealthy and middle-class people (sometimes collectively called "the owning class" because they hold property), working class and poor people. Sometimes this also includes the "barrier class," people who protect property and the owning class but are not necessarily part of the owning class themselves (the barrier class would include police and security forces).[14] The biggest divide is between folks who have the cushion of property ownership and folks

---

[14]A great intro resource to delve deeper into anti-classism is https://classism. org/about-class/what-is-classism/. I have also received excellent training on classism from *Think Again Training* (https://www.thinkagaintraining.com) and the Aorta Collective (https://aorta.coop/).

who don't, but class is also about more than just how much wealth you have.[15]

Class is largely about wealth, but each class also participates in setting and engaging the largely unspoken cultural rules and norms of a community—what's viewed as acceptable and what's not. Sometimes those rules have to do with a community's ethnic/racial makeup, but there are unspoken rules in multiracial communities with a shared class background.

One of the differences between wealthy and middle-class cultures is that middle-class people *practice* the norms; people of wealth might enforce cultural norms, but they also *shape* those cultural norms. Here is a rarefied example: the "health and wellness" company Goop's customers are middle and upper middle class, but the culture of Goop was shaped and molded by Gwyneth Paltrow, whose life experience, values, and priorities are shaped by her significant wealth. So, the values and priorities that her customers seek to emulate are shaped by a different class with access to different resources.

What's perhaps most interesting to me is that, while you would think that the middle class would resent or reject unattainable, decontextualized norms of the wealthier classes, more often than not, *the middle class functions as gatekeepers for the upper class*. In order for people with resources to retain their resources, certain stories need to be repressed. I'm not saying this is a conscious thing or some formalized conspiracy by the Storytelling Industrial Complex. What I'm suggesting is that over time, people with some means but also some financial precarity learned that their status in the world would be more secure if they blended in rather than stuck out. Over time, they learned not to tell stories that questioned how things are too much. They created barriers to the next generations' access to ancestors who fell outside the norm of their chosen society. They used story redaction to protect their property and reinforce who deserved access to it and who did not. Who did not were the troublemakers (the folks in the resistance stories).

---

[15]Wealth, in this context in particular, is about more than cash on hand. It's about the value of your assets minus the amount of your debts. The deep economic inequalities in the United States are fed by both the reduced value of the assets available to some people (lower wages, entrance to some professions, cost of education), the lack of inherited assets for some, and the debt load folks with less income of inherited wealth are required to take on to access higher income.

The sad result is that people in the middle class or aspiring to the middle class lose the stories of the resistors in their own families. They forget who they're connected to and what power they could take from those stories—stories of overcoming, resisting, and surviving. Stories of illicit hijinks and daring escapes. Stories of doing things differently than society told them were acceptable—the "counter-stories" which disrupt and reframe the dominant stock stories. *You* know. The *fun* stories.

> **What are the hidden stories in your family's history? Are there ways your family has benefited from stock stories? Were any of them part of resistance stories? How might you be carrying on a legacy by joining in the emerging stories today?**

When you have less to lose, there's sometimes more room for the whole story rather than just the stock story, especially if the stock story never had much to offer you in the first place. In that place, you might be in a better position to learn to whom you are really connected.

❦❦❦❦❦   ❦❦❦❦❦

I have been struck by the ways that wealth, class, caste, and gender have all figured into the stories my own extended family tells and doesn't tell.

I spent a summer volunteering at an HIV clinic in Kolkata in my late 20s. It was partly ministry training and partly to finally learn the language I had been around but never learned— Bengali. During that summer, an aunty showed me the photographs from her trip to the Andaman Islands. She explained that during the struggle for Indian independence, the fiercest revolutionaries and most visionary thinkers were sent there. She showed me photos of the cellular jail. She told me I would love it.

I convinced my parents to go to India with me that winter, and I suggested we visit the Andaman Islands. "Why would we do that?" my father asked, genuinely puzzled. "That's where the criminals were sent." I got the impression he had been raised with it as a threat over his head: "If you don't behave, the British will take you to the cellular jail," or something like that. So, I tried a reframe. "Have you heard of Robin Island?" He had. He knew it was the prison where Nelson Mandela was sent during

South African apartheid. "Well," I explained, "the Andaman Islands were our Robin Island."

We had an amazing trip, and I can't quite put into words how awe-inspiring it was to see so many Bengali names carved into the walls that honored everyone who had been imprisoned in that far-flung outpost during the height of the British reign.

While my father was ten when India celebrated independence, his education would have been a largely colonized one, with books provided by the British, with cultural values and tests created by the British, and with history narrated by the British. As a result, he was in his late sixties before he knew about one of the most powerful testaments to the freedom-fighting spirit of Indians and particularly Bengalis.

Sometimes our embarrassing ancestors are part of our resistance stories, which is exactly why they've been withheld from us. Sometimes stories are hidden unintentionally, masked by the different assumptions of social class.

My father's father was a Brahmin who was the headmaster of the village school because with an eighth grade education he was the most educated person in the village. My grandfather had three children: my father, as well another son and a daughter. When my father was a young man, he left India for an education and a future overseas, while the other two remained.

My cousins and I have wonderful relationships, though we have had very different experiences. As it turns out, we have also been told very different stories about our shared family tree. When I visited in 2019 to place my father's ashes in the Ganges, we began to see just how different.

My father had a great deal more opportunity to succeed professionally and economically in the UK and later the US than his siblings, but that's not to say it was always (or often) easy. When my parents first met, he was a PhD student and she was an elementary school teacher. Needless to say, they learned to manage with very little money. They also managed with less money than other schoolteacher/PhD student couples, because any money they didn't spend could go back to my aunt's family in India. My godmother tells of a grocery store trip, during which my mother grew frustrated that the store didn't have carrots with the tops still on. Unable to figure out all the fuss, my godmother said, "They cost the same, and you're just going to throw the tops away anyhow."

My mother explained that actually she needed the tops to make an extra meal that week: carrot top curry. She was counting on getting an extra meal out of what others might as easily throw away, in service to the extended family's economic well-being.

Of course, economic hardship was just the beginning. During that 2019 trip to India I talked about the racial bias my father lived through. My cousins, my uncle's children, were saddened and surprised. They hadn't realized the complexity of my father's experience. I said, "well, most immigrants don't go to another country because they're pulled by the allure of another place. They're usually pushed out of their home by violence or economic need." They were stunned by this.

The reason they were stunned is they had gotten a different, or at least a partial story. The story my uncle, a middle-class man, told was that he and others had sacrificed to send my father west to seek his fortune and make a new life. Which was *absolutely* true. But concealed in that narrative is the additional truth: my father was *sent* so he would have higher earning potential to help support his sister's family.

It's funny. My other cousins, my aunt's children, knew this. They grew up poor. They knew they didn't need to feel ashamed about that. They knew that my mother and father loved them so much that they wanted to help my aunt's family have more comfort and opportunity than they were able to access. So, my aunt and her family told that deeper story to each other and to their children. They treated my mother like blood family because that's what family does for each other—invest in each other fully.

My aunt's children are thriving and doing so much good in the world and have raised amazing and successful children. But growing up poor meant all the stories were on the table. Nothing to lose?

My uncle's family grew up with a little more than his sister's, though they too had responsibilities and supported my aunt's children. In addition to money, however, my uncle's children grew up in a different class experience; in town rather than a village, in our home region rather than in a different state with a different language, socializing with other middle-income people for the most part. Thus, struggling or facing bias didn't show up in the stories that got passed down. Their experience and the values of their context entailed acceptability, respectability, and adherence to norms.

It's not that my uncle's family thought there was shame in my aunt's family struggles per se, but to face a level of poverty that requires sending a family member away for the sake of the family back home requires confronting the conditions of a country where my aunt's husband worked for the government (on the railroads) and could not support his family with that job. Either that, or it requires blaming the family (particularly my aunt's husband) or even the grandfather who arranged the marriage to someone who couldn't earn a middle class income. Better to diminish that story and tell a more impressive story of an uncle who got to go west to live his best life.

In any number of communities, people tend to identify with the group they aspire to belong to, especially when it comes to class. That dynamic isn't particularly new: you can see it even in the Christian texts, and with particular clarity in James, one of the shorter New Testament books. If James was identifying pull quotes in his writing, his statement "Faith without works is dead" (2:17 KJV) would probably get the bigger print. But there are other gems, too. One recurring theme is the admonition to stop treating the rich people better than the poor people.

> James, 2,000 years ago, basically evoked the famous coal miners' strike song of the 1920s: "Which side are you on?"

I've read one passage a million times (James 2:1-10), preached on it too, and I always thought of it as a message about how God doesn't want us to discriminate. I read it again recently, and James actually says the reason we shouldn't treat rich people better than poor people is that poor people haven't done anything to make our lives worse, but rich people have. The rich charge us extortionate rents and lie about us in court so they can destroy our lives. We shouldn't mistreat poor people in the church, he says, because we have more in common with them than we'll ever have with rich people. James basically, 2,000 years ago evoked the famous coal miners' strike song of the 1920s: "Which side are you on?"

Whatever your spirituality or religion, James might be a good spiritual ancestor to claim. He did not want the stock story to be the only story.

He wanted the concealed story to be revealed and proclaimed, and for it to lead to resistance stories.

My experience reading James—of hearing, first, one meaning before realizing something else was also at work—has impacted the way I hear other stories, particularly stories that involve women.

On my 2019 visit to India, I went to see the village where my father was born, his mother's village. My family also took me to my grandfather's village and we were able to spend time with his youngest brother who followed the family tradition as Brahmins more literally and became a practicing Hindu priest. From memory, he took us back at least five generations of men in my family, including the very exciting-to-us fact that we had an ancestor four generations back who was a priest at the ancient and famous Dakeshwari Mandir in what is now Bangladesh.

Almost none of my family's documented ancestry includes the women. We trace our stories through the men. In fact, my family got frustrated with how much I wanted to spend time in my grandmother's village where our parents were born and grew up. Why, they wondered, didn't I feel more affinity for my grandfather's village (where most of our in-laws grew up)?

I recently talked with a couple of colleagues, one a Korean American woman and one a Kenyan American man. They asked me about this book, and the woman shared some ancestral practices she loves that are frowned on because they're pre-Christian and considered dangerous by the Christian majority. Then she asked her friend whether he had any ancestral practices. "Yeahhhhhhh," he said slowly, looking for the right words. He began by pointing out, "This is the most western conversation I can imagine," before explaining that in his place of birth, every man in his village had a tree planted where they were buried, and they continued to contribute to the life of the village after death. The trees bore the names they had in life. This disconnection from ancestors felt, to him, like a decidedly American issue.

My fragile wounded self was about to comment that his village must have gotten the chillest missionaries, but before I could, my colleague said, "just the men, huh?" He nodded solemnly, very aware of whose stories were romanticized and whose stories were overlooked, even amidst such a powerful practice to continue learning from ancestors.

When we are taught to overlook whole genders, whole castes, whole religious traditions, we want to be mindful, when finally engaging their stories once more, not to collapse those individuals with their stories and complexities into overly simple categories and experiences.

One of the best sermons I have ever heard was by the Rev. Dr. Donna Allen at the beginning of a national conference of Christian activists engaged in the Movement for Black Lives, in January 2016 at First Congregational Church of Oakland. Her sermon was on the story from the Jewish sacred text of Genesis, about the patriarch Abram, his wife Sarai and Hagar, the woman they enslaved.

I will note from the beginning that the text very carefully treats the story as if it is a squabble between women where the man bears no responsibility even though he holds absolute power. Dr. Allen's point, however, was the way in which God's orientation towards liberation got erased from the text in order to justify the stock story of Abram's goodness as well as God's goodness. The text says that when Sarai becomes jealous that Hagar is pregnant with Abram's baby, Hagar flees, and then the Angel of God makes her return.

Dr. Allen asked the audience how many of us believe that God is a God of liberation. The whole crowd said *yes*. She said the God she worships would not send an enslaved person back to slavery, so we could see that the true story had been glossed over. As best my memory serves, she said, "so we know what really would have happened. She fled, and Abram sent guards to capture her. When they did, she said, 'Oh, OK; this was my reconnaissance mission. Now I know the lay of the land for the next time I leave.'"

In a story where Abram is overromanticized and protected by a stock story for the sake of patriarchy, the overlooked stories of both Hagar and Sarai teach us something about who we are and whose we are. Even though Sarai behaves horribly in this story, she is constrained by the patriarchy and has very few options. She then chooses to use those limited choices and power to harm the person who falls below her in the hierarchy, likely because her grasp on a small modicum of power is so tenuous, which is a lesson for us all; but it's worth paying attention to the complexities of these characters and their contexts.

Similarly, the remarkable diversity and complexity of Indigenous people and communities in the United States are often collapsed into homogenous stock stories. In these stories, Indigenous people are made to play the role of wizened spiritual leaders, victims of oppression, and a noble, if eradicated, presence in the history of white Americans.

I was listening to a radio show hosted by, and featuring guests who were, Native American activists and scholars. They noted that one of their greatest frustrations, to a person, was the way non-Native people talked about them as if they were not still alive and in community and with wisdom to offer. They discussed how much of that had to do with US education and imagery in the media; our children learn a story about the first Thanksgiving, some about Native spirituality, and maybe even about the Trail of Tears. But there is always a sense that those people are gone now. That they have no descendants. That whatever their place in the story, they are no more. The guests on the show agreed that the result was people could paint romantic (and inaccurate) images of their ancestors, while simultaneously denying the Native people right in front of them.

Stock stories of dominance tend to value flat characterization of the long dead over complex, living communities, as well as a sense of purity over the very real, and quite pervasive, intermingling of peoples and culture. Stock stories presume that our ancestors lived in cultural vacuums, not universes.

Those stock stories are powerful in shaping our self-perception: the people who matter have clear, undiluted, pure bloodlines. As I told a friend about this project on linking to our ancestors, just as I was getting started with my research, he replied, "OK, but what if I'm just a mutt?" I didn't realize then how many times I would hear variations on that question over the next several years. *What about the rest of us? The ones whose ancestors weren't the history makers, the kings and queens? Is our importance as diluted as our bloodlines?*

I empathize with my friend's concern, but the truth behind the stock story is this: many, if not most, of us have had our ancestral ties disrupted. Even our romanticized ancestors face that challenge. In the dramatic series *The Crown* (Netflix), there is a scene where Prince Phillip's mother, Princess Alice, warns her brother Lord Mountbatten not to think he has the right to claim Britain as his country to rule, saying, "We Battenberg may have kings and queens in our line, but we're mongrels, too. Part German, part Greek, part nowhere-at-all."[16]

Henry Louis Gates once did an entire episode of *Finding Your Roots* on Black celebrities who were certain they had Native ancestors. While only one of the eight did, Gates emphasized the greater truth (and subliminally political message of his show):

> And I think that the political -- the subliminal political messages of *Finding Your Roots* each week are, one, that we're 99.9 percent the same, no matter where we came from. And, two, there is no such thing as racial purity. Our use of genetics deconstructs the racist notions of white supremacists, that there is -- that we're all pure, that we're purely Black, that race is.[17]

My longtime friend Stepan got a DNA test a while ago. While Indigenous/ Native American DNA didn't show up as a huge percentage, it was larger than average for someone who was also the son of a Daughter of the American Revolution. Stepan knows that using DNA as a cultural marker is an ambiguous thing at best and that due to the dual strategies of active genocide and cultural genocide through intermarriage, many people who are part of Indigenous communities today do not have incredibly high percentages of "Indigenous DNA." Maybe even less than Stepan. Perhaps because he knew that, Stepan noted his test results with interest but didn't give it too much thought.

Then, he received a box that his recently deceased father had left for him. Amidst other artifacts were pictures of visibly Indigenous people with Stepan's father. Stepan remembered visiting them in childhood and his father giving them money and boxes of clothes. He had explained this as part of their church's mission work. But as Stepan looked at the photos, he realized for the first time that the people they had visited were his father's family. His father had actively hidden that fact in order to be accepted into a very conservative religious community as one of its prominent leaders. Stepan's DNA results made a bit more sense after this revelation.

Still, Stepan isn't choosing to fetishize this newfound part of his identity. He's seeking to honor it. He's seeking ways to honor it and to discern

---

[16]Dialogue from Episode 5, season 3 of the Crown
[17]http://edition.cnn.com/TRANSCRIPTS/2001/16/ampr.01.html

whether there are healthy ways to build relationship with the Indigenous community to which his ancestors belonged. He lives near one but had previously been told that even if he was in the market for an Indigenous community to claim him, they might well decline to do so.

He remains as aware as ever of how often connections to Indigeneity get abused by people for whom Indigenous people are an abstraction, while the reality of overlooked (and in this case actively hidden) Indigenous ancestors holds more powerful and more painful truths than the romanticizing done by people with no relationship to the Indigenous people in their midst.

I have a lot more work to do to connect with the overlooked ancestors in my own family's story. Someone who gives me a lot of inspiration for how to do that is, ironically, neither Hindu nor South Asian: the scholar Wendy Doniger. In her controversial but well-researched book *The Hindus: An Alternative History*, Doniger notes that for millennia women, people of marginalized classes and castes, and people of other religions have influenced ancient written texts and oral traditions (since innovative thinking happens among both people with education and without). She explains that sometimes you can see their influence in the things the texts say that weren't the prevalent thinking at the time. Sometimes you can see their influence because of a glitch in the text that means something was erased or taken out. And sometimes you can see their influence because the text is overemphatic in its rejection of said women, poor people or people from non-dominant castes.[18]

One example Doniger provides is that of Raikva, a mystic in the ancient Hindu text the Upanishads. Raikva is the first houseless person in world literature. "An understanding of the social context of the Upanishads," Doniger writes, "reintroducing the world into the text, may go a long way to explain not who first thought of the story of Raikva, but why the Brahmins were willing to include his story in their texts despite the ways in which it challenged their social order."[19]

There's a gift in unearthing stories of people who came before who didn't fit the mold. I am connected to a weeklong program specifically for

---

[18]She also notes that there have always been many Hinduisms, and the effort to pretend there is one uniform Hinduism is another effort at the erasure of important but often overlooked voices.

[19]Doniger, Wendy, *The Hindus, An Alternative History.* p. 21.

young South Asian activists. During the week of their stay, these young activists learn the organizing and communication skills needed to launch a social justice campaign. They also learn about globalization, workers' rights, and other justice issues. The first thing they experience, though, is a timeline of South Asians in the US. They learn about artists who collaborated with Black leaders in the Harlem Renaissance. They learn about LGBTQ+ South Asians organizing in the 1970s and 80s. They learn about taxicab worker strikes for decent living conditions and farmers who have lived in this country for over 100 years despite always being called foreigners. They learn about Dalit[20] women leading a campaign to take down a businessman who was trafficking Dalit women from his village in India to work in his restaurant in Berkeley.

Some of the youth come from poverty or from lower castes. Many of them are middle class (even if struggling middle class), and also privileged castes, with a lot of social pressures to follow a very specific path in order to fit in and establish a certain career so that they do not embarrass the family. The timeline helps them see for the first time that throughout the history of this country there have been South Asians like them: South Asians who care about justice, who have struggled for dignity but not for conformity, who are in solidarity with Black and Latine and Indigenous people and not only aspiring to a certain type of proximity to whiteness.

The sad thing is that far too often these young activists have to step away from their family and community in order to experience this narrative. The beautiful thing is that once they learn the truth of this history, they feel a sense of connection to something broader than their families of origin. Those may not be their biological ancestors, but they are absolutely their spiritual ancestors, or as I call them, their movement ancestors. Connecting to the resistance stories helps them find how they can be part of their own emerging or transforming stories to carry on those ancestors' legacies, even at the annoyance or outrage of their biological family.

Here's the thing about our ancestors: we may have had ancestors who were royalty. We may have had ancestors who were brutally oppressed.

---

[20]Dalit is generally the preferred term for people from the Hindu tradition who fall outside the caste system and are treated in an inferior way, including being assigned work deemed too "unclean" for people of any other caste.

For most of us, we have ancestors who lived to work another day, who sought to make sure their families had enough to eat, and who lived through some interesting history but did not necessarily play a role in it. We might pick up some of those stories regardless of our class background: people on the frontier, people who were forced here or who came here because of economic conditions in the homeland, people who faced adversity and survived it. We may even get to hear about the bootlegger or the businessman whose business was a threat to the bigwigs in town and so it was destroyed. The stories of people who were not challenging the system per se or who were somehow socially acceptable in how they challenged power—those stories can stay, generally.

That said, there are stories we may not get to hear because those stories threaten the status quo in some way.

They will be hard to unearth.

We will have to develop the skills of listening to the message hidden between the lines. Wendy Doniger is a master at this. She can point out where Dalits and women and poor people influenced ancient sacred Hindu texts and where the priests tried to erase them and where the texts show that their power was growing and so they were demonized as a result. This might be why the Hindu Nationalist Party destroyed every copy of her book, *The Hindus: An Alternative History,* in India and why she has received so many death threats from Hindu nationalists.

My friend Jeffrey has a last name that ties back to that story of Hagar—Ishmael, the name of Hagar's baby. Jeffrey shared with me one time where the name came from: his people are from the Kentucky-Indiana region of the US. Ishmael was a name *chosen* in opposition to the name Issac that was given to this Indigenous family when they were Christianized by Moravian missionaries. His people were a diverse bunch: Indigenous, Europeans who skipped out of their indenture, and Black people who had freed themselves from enslavement and found a home

· · · · · · · · · · · · · · · · · ·

If you want to hear an inspiring spoken word reflection on the ancestral power of names, and how the dominant culture tries to take away this power, you need to hear one by Zachary Caballero! Find "When You Say My Name" on YouTube.

together. Those three groups had chosen to become one community and one very extended family, surviving and living and loving as they seasonally and systematically roamed the Midwest for a century, an act of resistance against the dominant culture and also an act of commitment to their respective ways of understanding how community protects each other. They wanted a name that reflected not the beloved son Isaac, born to an oppressive couple, but instead the son of a mother who resisted, who persevered, who named God and made a way out of no way.

I love how Jeffrey's family takes what others might see as an embarrassing history and instead claims their ancestry as transformative and good. I am trying to do the same with one of my overlooked ancestors.

I have a cousin (my father's eldest niece by his sister) who married outside her caste. For doing so, she was largely cut out of the family narrative for decades because caste oppression runs so deep in our culture. I didn't know she existed until I was twenty because her marriage was such a source of shame for the family that she was functionally disowned and spoken of only in whispers.

At my father's nudging, some of her siblings reconnected with her (even though it felt like rejecting their parents' will and dishonoring their parents' heartbreak over having to disown her). I did get to spend time with her and her children on a visit in my late twenties. She has since died, and she now exists to me as an ancestor, a too-long overlooked ancestor that I imagine at least some of my cousins' children still don't know about.

Even if you've read Isabelle Wilkerson's book *Caste*, caste is still an abstraction to you if you're not South Asian. Wilkerson used caste as a powerful, apt metaphor, but still a metaphor that cannot capture the reality of what it means to live in a culture shaped so profoundly by caste. I wrestle to understand its impact in my life, knowing how deeply it has affected my ancestors and living family alike, knowing that it still benefits me in this country. Yet, I am allowed to ignore it if I choose, because I live in a land that only knows it as a metaphor, and because of my caste privilege.

I am spending time these days thinking about the stories my father left me about where caste caused harm as a way of getting to the concealed stories beneath the stock story. I'm also thinking about what it means to turn to my cousin intentionally as an ancestor who participated in a resistance story by marrying the person she loved, moving to another community, and choosing a new beginning and a new narrative of who she was and whose she was.

As I think about my cousin as ancestor, it connects me in new ways to stories of my Scottish mother, not yet an ancestor, who had to make some of the same choices for marrying outside her race and religion. I grew up with many family traditions that weren't actually ancestral family traditions. When my mother was cut out of her parents' narrative, she created new traditions with her new family, and she adopted some of my father's traditions as well.

The hidden stories of your ancestors may take a lot of forms. Perhaps your embarrassing ancestors caused trouble and stuck out and were therefore erased. Perhaps the overlooked ancestors were the people who survived and endured or who otherwise extricated themselves from the narrative in order to live free. *Hamilton* fans will remember Alexander's betrayed and heartbroken wife Eliza burning her letters as she sings *I'm erasing myself from the narrative . . .* Sometimes the only way to escape the constraints of other people's narratives is to leave entirely.

Those ancestors may have influenced and shaped stories, but over time their contributions were eroded because they didn't serve the dominant narrative told by people with power. Those ancestors may have been reconcilers or persuaders or community-builders in a world that knows better what to do with stories about and lives directed by demagogues and conquerors and commanders.

This is why it is so important for us to work to uncover the hidden stories of our ancestors. Their complex realities and the mundane details of their lives help us to keep them alive and discourage us from dismissing them as historical artefacts. Most of us have nothing in common with royal ancestors, but we can piece together the possibilities and challenges of a peasant or a housewife or someone facing debt. Our overlooked ancestors might have navigated similar terrain to ours and have models or cautionary tales.

Our overlooked ancestors can also point us to the real dangers we face rather than the made-up dangers meant to distract us. For example, our economic exploitation is real. The threat to us from people of another culture is much less statistically real regardless of our culture or the other culture involved.

Finally, our overlooked ancestors remind us of where we come from and why that invites us into solidarity with people around us also facing struggles.

In the last chapter of my book *Transforming Communities: How People Like You are Healing Their Neighborhoods*, I tell the story of the village of Le Chambon, France. In that chapter, I say that their magic was in knowing who you are in order to be whom you need to be. In other words, internalize your story so that it shapes how you engage the world.

Le Chambon itself was as overlooked as its ancestors. Then, in the 1930s, Alexandre Trocme arrived as their village pastor with a dream of creating a pacifist community due to his experiences as a child during World War I. Almost the whole village could trace their roots back to the Huguenots, Protestants who had been forced out of a Catholic France hundreds of years prior and still lived mostly on its edges. Every week, Pastor Trocme reminded them who they were and whose they were, and what that meant.

So, when intellectuals and others fleeing the fascist regime in Spain found their way to Le Chambon, the village protected them and led them to safety because the descendants of Huguenots understand persecution. That understanding led them to understand themselves as *those who help the persecuted*. Later, when Jews and others began arriving as they fled the Nazi regime, the village protected them and led them to safety, too, because the descendants of Huguenots understand persecution, *which means they help the persecuted*. And when France fell to the Vichy government, the village nonviolently resisted the Vichy government, because the descendants of Huguenots understand persecution, *which means they resist the persecutors*. That's all pretty miraculous in and of itself, but those folks also managed to both resist their persecutors and simultaneously treat them as if they were children of God.

In other words, our overlooked ancestors can help us learn about injustice in the past. It is our job to connect it to what happens in the present.

Whether we had tattie howkers in our family tree or dowager duchesses or princes from this land or lands faraway, the task ahead of us is to surface the stories of resistance that this world is afraid of and to be aware of where we benefit from certain stock stories at the expense of our historic legacies. In doing that work, we may discover that we are truer inheritors of troublemaking ancestors than we were ever allowed to believe.

Where We Can Go From Here

○ *If you want to write and reflect on this chapter's theme in your own life:*

Think of a story of a great hero in history. Write about the people who probably made their success possible but who got left out of the narrative. Or write about a major historic event and think of all the people whose names we don't know who contributed to it. Give thanks for them.

○ *If you want to engage a personal ritual around this chapter's theme:*

I've been exploring the possibility that there are four different types of people necessary to the social justice movement, many of whom get overlooked even though we need them all. Locate *yourself*:

- Mystic (tapped into that which is beyond us)
- Mourner (who grieves our losses and what has caused them)
- Prophet (who points us in the direction of wholeness)
- Reveler (who creates joy in order to keep us going)

Recognize there are ancestors of each type. Give gratitude to them if you don't know them yet, even if their stories have been hidden, that you might connect with them.

○ *If you want to engage your activist or spiritual group in a practice that will help them begin to connect with ancestors in new ways as part of their work to dismantle white supremacy:*

Share with each other your favorite overlooked ancestor. Write down on a piece of paper a word to describe what you value about them. Create an altar by laying the pieces of paper down and lighting a candle in the midst of them, to express gratitude for their no longer overlooked contributions to our world today. Have someone read each of the words out loud and have the group respond (e.g. if someone's piece of paper says "tenacity," the leader would say "for the gift of our ancestors' tenacity," and the group would respond "we are grateful.")

○ *Bonus*

If you want to go deeper on your own: Read Ron Takaki's *A Different Mirror* or Howard Zinn's *A People's History of the United States*. Where do you see your people in their fullness, no longer overlooked?

Chapter Three

Atrocious Ancestors

When my ancestors came from Africa, they were shackled by our neck, our wrists, and our ankles in steel chains. I've turned those steel chains into gold to symbolize the fact that I'm still a slave, only my price tag is higher.

—Mr. T

In my social justice work, I have noticed that when people doing the hard work of justice in the streets have a deep connection to ancestors, they were more motivated to stay in the work. I have also noticed that as my colleagues brought ancestral rituals into protests, it changed the energy in the group for the better. This made sense to me since I had seen the same thing in interfaith justice work.

When I was first doing that work, I was driven mainly by a desire to help people connect to those tools—for religious groups timid about justice work to realize they had amazing gifts of ritual from their ancestors to embolden them, and for folks deep in the work of justice to tap into those same gifts, so they experienced support and encouragement and felt more grounded in the work (and less prone to burnout).

I didn't realize at the time that I also brought a very optimistic framework for who our ancestors were or that I had overromanticized mine in some dangerous ways. I've noted that many resistance stories are erased by people trying to blend in as a survival tool. You'll hear me say in future chapters that we also need to connect to the stories of our working-class ancestors as part of staying grounded (just as our justice work today needs to remain connected to working people). I also buy into what I think of as the 99 percent theory of ancestors: very few of us come from the 1 percent, the elite, the very wealthy. So, we may have (and if we're thinking intersectionally, most of us have) had ancestors who participated in or propped up oppression, but the odds of us being at the top of the pyramid? Very, very low. We have more in common with the serfs than the lairds in Scotland, more in common with the rice harvesters than with the zamindars in India.

You may already see where this was all about to go sideways.

In the early stages of researching this book, I was invited to help facilitate a three-day retreat on racial justice. During the retreat, I led an optional workshop about how connecting with spiritual and cultural practices of ancestors leads to dismantling white supremacy. In the description of the workshop, I emphasized that I was trying out a theory, and I had no answers.

About twenty people attended. I did my welcome and explained that most of us come from common stock. We would need to do the work of empathy with ancestors doing the best they could to survive, but also the work of learning from where they may have sided with the oppressor, thinking it would lift them up instead of staying in solidarity with other oppressed people.

Then I asked why people had come to this workshop. Three of them said because they had enslavers in their ancestry, and they didn't know what to do with it.

Oh.

Despite my 99 percent ancestors theory, it turns out about 6 percent of the free population of enslaving states actively enslaved people, and they were, not surprisingly, almost all white. That's already a high number. And that's only counting the people who were the enslavers on paper (usually the patriarch). Including their family, about 30 percent of people in enslaving states, again almost all white, were part of an immediate family that enslaved people.[21] So, the people in that workshop were not a statistical fluke.

---

[21]https://socialequity.duke.edu/wp-content/uploads/2020/08/8.10.20.pdf

Maybe it's because I hang out with so many people of color, but I had drastically discounted the number of people, especially in white communities, with what I call in this chapter "atrocious ancestors." This is just one place where our own social location as descendants of these varied ancestors will shape the work we have to do.

It is not only people with enslavers in their family tree who confront hard questions about atrocious ancestors. About twenty years ago, I came upon a series of resources about the descendants of high-ranking members of the Third Reich. One or two became popular figures in the neo-Nazi movement, several sought to avoid thinking about or in any way affiliating with that history, and several had become vehement and public opponents of anti-Semitism. Among that last group, one woman spent most of her elder years co-leading youth tours of the death camp where her father had been commandant, talking about the need to know the ugly past in order to create a better future, at the invitation of and alongside a Holocaust survivor.

Neither is this a challenge only for white Westerners. When I first began talking about this book, a colleague of mine followed me downstairs from a meeting to snag me in the lobby of her office building to have a whispered conversation with me.

"You travel in the same progressive South Asian organizing circles as I do," she said hurriedly before people noticed she was missing at work. "And you know everyone says Hinduism is uniquely irredeemable."

I had heard that phrase repeated from multiple sources in our organizing: "uniquely irredeemable." It's usually paired with another phrase that explains why people call it that: "Brahminical patriarchy."

Now, both adherents and scholars will sometimes defend Christianity by arguing that its evils and failings are the results of western imperialism. So, too, the harms done by the modern state of Israel can be blamed on the oppressed becoming the oppressor or the complications of twentieth-century global politics, and, probably, western imperialism. Whatever the cause, the prevailing sense is that the religion itself, the core of belief and practice, is not to blame.

Hinduism, in the eyes of my colleague, is different. Before the British, before the Mughals, Hinduism had thousands of years of casteism and gender oppression baked into it from its very origins. Violence towards women and non-dominant castes and non-caste people is not just a byproduct, the argument goes, but a foundation. For those of us who are the descendants of that ancient line of priests, what did our ancestors oversee? Tolerate? Advocate for? From sati, the ancient practice of burning the bride on her dead husband's funeral pyre, to blessing the theft of Indigenous land and beyond, the possibilities are heartbreaking.

The reason she followed me downstairs for that fragment of a conversation was because she hoped with all her heart Hinduism wasn't uniquely irredeemable and she knew I have a passion for Hindu liberation ethics (akin to the Black and Latine liberation theologies of Christianity), but she also knew that her ancestors had caused enough pain that she wasn't necessarily the best arbiter of that decision. Nor was I.

That same struggle arose when my colleague BK and I used to teach a course (now available online) about self-care and community care for the sake of the social justice movement. When the course was held at Allen Temple, a Black Baptist church with a long history of social justice work in the community, we would invite local activists and organizers who engage in embodiment and mindfulness as part of their social justice work. I will never forget when our incredible colleague, Katie, generously talked about their grandparents from mixed backgrounds, Black and Jewish. They shared that their Jewish grandfather survived the Nazi death camps by lending his valuable mechanic skills to the Nazis in exchange for his life. This led Katie to wonder, "how many good people didn't make it out?" Katie wasn't saying their grandfather was a bad person. They weren't saying to the students that their ancestors who survived enslavement were bad. They were saying that horrific circumstances force people to make horrific choices, which in turn caused damage.

Part of the work of social justice, of telling and living transformative stories, is becoming a community that can validate and support others who may be descended from a line of "atrocious ancestors." In fact, we have to confront the horrors our ancestors wrought, and we are far more likely to do so in productive ways with the help of those around us.

One of the most helpful exercises I ever engaged in regarding that challenge was one my beloved friend, Cisa Payuyo, posed when she and I were working together on a workshop on ancestors designed for people of color. She had the group consider this question: "Think of an ancestor that you need to tell, 'You did [this thing] wrong.' What do you need to tell them?"

I think the reason this was such a powerful question to me is because of a conversation I had with a colleague years before. He was doing some really beautiful work to help Black people grieve, mourn, and process loss through ritual, and to seek encouragement and support from their ancestors. In passing, I said, "Yeah...some of us have jerks for ancestors."

He smiled and said, "Right. That's why we have to help them become better ancestors."

My colleague was a Black queer man in the church. His ancestors had created some of the conditions that cause pain in his life. It would have been absolutely understandable for him to say, "Right, so we cut them out."

There are powerful ancient rituals that allow people to cut cords with ancestors causing them pain. That is absolutely a thing. I have seen the Celtic version of the cord-cutting ritual provide healing and freedom.

But my colleague had decided that while his ancestors might rightly deserve being cut off, he wanted to give them a chance at something else. (This, by the way, is what Christians call grace.)

As we encounter ancestors, especially atrocious ancestors, we are called on to ask *who we are* as well as *who they were*. (If my colleague is right, we might also think about who they are and who they could be). Cisa offers a bold vision of confronting ancestors head-on. My colleague offers a vision for helping them be something better. Both of them come from cultures that are committed to family connections even when those connections are complicated and painful. That commitment is evident in the ways that they seek to engage ancestors.

Another friend of mine, Bentley, comes out of what we would call the dominant culture. In one of our wisdom circles, he shared a story about his stepfather, now passed away. His stepfather did a lot of things that stand directly against the work Bentley dedicates himself as an active anti-racist. He played a key role in the most racist of the Nixon administration's agenda, for example. At the same time, Bentley's father-in-law was also a loving man.

Bentley mentioned that these days, because his stepfather loved to cook, when he cooks, he spends time listening to his stepfather's spirit. Just listening. Because Bentley is clear on which beliefs and actions of his stepfather were wrong, and because foundationally Bentley is someone who believes in the potential goodness of every human being, Bentley has found space in his heart in this season to create space for his stepfather to speak, heal, and contribute to something healthier now than he did in life. Bentley's practice is one way of helping our ancestors be better ancestors. It is born of the belief that few people are wholly atrocious, which makes things messy and difficult and also potential-filled.

I don't have an answer as to whether some of our ancestors are irredeemable, or whether they can be confronted as part of our process of healing. But I do know that I've brought questions and frustrations and even criticisms to ancestors in my prayers and meditations, and it has helped me feel clearer and less mired down. Sometimes in those conversations I've discovered I'm talking to middlemen, and sometimes I'm talking to people who chose badly because they had only bad options to choose from.

In the previous chapter, I talked briefly about purity and bloodlines and the fact that a lot of us self-identify somewhat shamefacedly as mutts. Remembering that there's not much in reality that looks like "racial purity," we can wrestle with these ideas in the hope that doing so might help us re-encounter atrocious ancestors in new ways.

My beloved colleague and brother from another mother, Jose, hails from Puerto Rico, a country whose history is rife with colonization. It includes genocide against the Taino people. It includes enslaved Black people and Black people who liberated themselves. Jose quotes scholar Justo Gonzalez when he describes the Boriquen[22] experience this way: "We have both the blood of the colonized and of the colonizer in our veins."

When I asked my friend Ayanna what it was like for her to spend a term in Ghana when she was in college, she shared a lot of powerful memories. The one that has stayed with me was the fact that everyone in Ghana

---

[22]The Taino people indigenous to Puerto Rico referred to island as **Boriquén**. This is why Puerto Rico is now also called Borinquen by Puerto Rican people.

could immediately recognize Ayanna as an American. Though Ayanna does not consider herself mixed race—she is a Black woman—she noted that no one in Ghana has skin as light as hers. Most Black and Indigenous people in the US, most enslaved and many colonized people, have mixed bloodlines that were not of their ancestors' choosing.

The terms "mixed race," "biracial" or that ugly, old, institutional term "miscegenated" are usually meant to talk about people like me, and particularly people with one white parent and another parent who is a person of color, usually (although not always) a pairing of choice. There aren't terms for the people with a more dispersed lineage, one they can't trace easily, one erased by the violence of enslavement or colonization or cultural genocide and the sexual violence that often accompanies it. White supremacy culture doesn't really have a way of referring to its ongoing erasure of other cultures.

Given the fact that many more of us may have connections to atrocious ancestors than we previously thought, how might we begin the work of confronting them?

It's likely that anyone who has taken a class or a course or a training or a workshop with me has heard me quote Adrienne Maree Brown, author of *Emergent Strategy* and editor of *Holding Change*. I claim her because she has logged in many hours in Oakland and with Oaklanders I love. But it wasn't until I read the essay she wrote a month after George Floyd's murder that I learned we are both bi-racial. Her expansive, generous, and direct essay, "A Word for White People in Two Parts," is worth a full reading, but for our purposes, I want to hone in on a particularly direct portion where she evokes ancestors.

> Your ancestors did not fight fair, and they didn't teach you to be in right relationship with anyone. They didn't give our ancestors time to wonder, ask for help, course correct, or negotiate. This is why some say you should be grateful we seek justice, equality, and our humanity, versus revenge. Because right now, after years of physical, intellectual and cultural warfare on peoples who were different from white, you have an opportunity to leap forward, dive into this river of change, rather than be deluged and drowned in it.
>
> The time for denial is over. You were not raised in a secret mountaintop retreat disconnected from the world; you haven't

existed with no contact for over 400 years . . . so we know you
see and know what is going on. And you're scared, saddened,
defensive, guilty, and unsure of who to be if you aren't the
default superior. So you make choices towards or away from
or against your own highest self.[23]

My friend (and co-pastor forever) Tai Amri shared in a wisdom circle
about a trip he got to take to Kenya. "I remember people being like
'You're not African. You should not call yourself African American.' There
was anger, but as I spent more time with them, I realized how much
misunderstanding we had about each other."

Tai Amri explained that his Kenyan colleagues felt abandoned, that
he and the other African Americans on the trip were the descendants
of people who went to the US and liked it so much they never came
back. He found it such a bizarre myth for people to have perpetuated,
and the outcome was to create division among people who should be
family. "Because we were in relationship, I was able to explain," he said,
but not everyone has the opportunity that Tai Amri had; they aren't
able to build relationships across that vast expanse of ocean, that vast
expanse of history, that vast expanse of pain. There are also African
Americans who carry the pain that even though they know that their
ancestors' enslavement was almost completely the result of European
imperialism and the newly emerging reality of white supremacy
culture, there were Africans involved in selling their ancestors to the
white men who propped up enslavement in Europe, the Caribbean
and the Americas.

I wrote a sermon, published in *Preaching as Resistance*, a year or so into
the Trump administration about a couple of my favorite Woody Guthrie
songs, both of which were about Jesus resisting greed, corporations, and
fascism. Guthrie is probably most famous for his song "This Land is Your
Land," which he wrote as a response to the dangerous jingoism of "God
Bless America." The most famous image of him is a photo of him holding
his guitar, onto which is carved the phrase "this machine kills fascists."

When I was researching that sermon, I discovered some horrifying
things about Woody Guthrie's father, Charles. You may already know
how violent the white supremacist movement was in the early 1900s

---

[23]https://adriennemareebrown.net/2020/06/28/a-word-for-white-people-
in-two-parts

in Oklahoma, where Woody Guthrie was born. His father was widely rumored to be involved in the lynching of a Black mother and son in 1911, and Woody Guthrie went on to write several songs about Charles's involvement with the burgeoning Ku Klux Klan at around the same time.

Woody Guthrie and his son Arlo would make careers protesting war, violence, fascism, and racism. Woody actively named the harm his father did, writing songs about his racist acts and affiliations, and dedicated his life to repudiating those horrors and building an alternative to them, a world of justice and equality. He reminds me of those children of Nazi leaders who chose to publicly disavow and to make repairs as best they could. I can imagine him engaging Cisa's question, and turning it into music that is also story, in order to help others find the courage to confront the atrocious ancestors in their family trees as well.

Some of us are facing the challenge of coming to terms with the very real existence of our ancestors who did horrific and violent harm, including enslavement, serving in a concentration camp, and more. Some of us are learning that we have ancestors who survived horrors beyond imagining and are learning how to be in relationship with them. Both challenges and learnings are difficult, but there seems to be some moral clarity in how to pursue that work. What do the rest of us do with a third group of ancestors, those who may have benefitted from oppression or suffered under it, but whose greatest sin was to tolerate evil, to take it for granted, perhaps not to even notice it? That's the group whose past complicity and inaction terrifies me; it is terrifying, particularly because I fear that many of us today might be doing the same thing.

I recently read a deep and expansive essay about Alice Walker and Flannery O'Connor growing up very near each other in Georgia, although O'Connor was Walker's senior, someone Walker studied in college until she discovered the Black women authors who had been withheld from her and turned to them instead. The essay acknowledges that even though the realities of our atrocious ancestors can be painful to us, the greatest harm is done by systems far greater than even the worst individual, and by the countless people who play a role in propping up that institutionalized evil.

In the essay, Walker describes taking her mother on a trip back to Georgia, years after making a life for herself in New York, to visit the falling remains of the house they once inhabited. While there, Walker goes to visit O'Connor's house as well. The article quotes Walker's description of the moment Walker knocked on O'Connor's door.

> She wrote of that moment: "It all comes back to houses. To how people live. There are rich people who own houses to live in and poor people who do not. And this is wrong. I think: I would level this country with a sweep of my hand, if I could."

> She called out the difference that race has made in the lives— and afterlives—of Black and white artists. In Mississippi, there is a house museum much like Andalusia for William Faulkner, but "no one even remembers where Richard Wright lived." This, however, was bearable to Walker.

> "What comes close to being unbearable," she wrote, "is that I know how damaging to my own psyche such injustice is. In an unjust society the soul of the sensitive person is in danger of deformity from just such weights as this. For a long time I will feel Faulkner's house, O'Connor's house, crushing me."[24]

I once co-taught a community organizing class with BK where we asked the students to break up into two groups and each group to name the foundational evil in the world against which we were called to fight. After much discussion and wrestling and nuancing and finally agreeing, both groups were ready to present.

One group said "greed." The other group said "fear."

We talked about how greed and fear feed into each other. While that course was back in 2016, I carry those two words with me everywhere. I see them everywhere. I see them leveraged against us constantly. I see politicians leaning on one or the other in order to pit us against each other. In our history, I see those twin evils playing themselves out in the decisions of our ancestors, causing them to sell each other out, too often quite literally. And I see those twin evils being leveraged against our ancestors, until the weight of those powers greater than them crushes them.

Flannery O'Connor benefited from so much privilege. As Walker noted, what is most horrific is the world around her that preserves Faulkner's

[24]https://bittersoutherner.com/two-houses-on-the-eatonton-milledgeville-road-flannery-oconnor-alice-walker

home (and O'Connor's) and not Richard Wright's. The point isn't that O'Connor was an atrocious ancestor, rather she lived in a world where atrocious ancestors made her success possible (even in the face of patriarchy). As we confront our ancestors, how do we pay attention to the systems they benefited from? How do we make sense of what they longed for, what they feared, that caused them to make the choices they made? How might that examination help us learn from their horrible examples? How do we learn from how a collective culture among our ancestors was atrocious, even if the individuals from our own genealogies were passive supporters or beneficiaries of it? How do we learn from the ways some of our ancestors benefitted from the atrocities, even as they named other injustices in their midst, as O'Connor and Faulkner did? Could that get us closer to understanding what our role is in our context today? What can we learn, we who hold certain unjust systems in contempt, and yet simultaneously benefit from them?

My friend Kaaryn noted that in her years of interfaith work, and through attendance at a variety of Jewish Passover Seders, she has been inspired by the ways that all the participants in a horrific long-ago event are named. A religious ritual that in and of itself is about honoring ancestors, many seders don't stop with the story from the book of Exodus where Moses led the Israelites out of bondage. Those seders include a recognition of what it means to deprive others of land in their pursuit of a safe haven after years of enslavement. Part of the ritual itself even names that God grieved for the deaths of the Pharaoh's soldiers who had brought such suffering into the lives of the Israelites. At those seders, the ritual names the plagues brought down on the enslaving nation in response to the atrocities they committed, but it also invites those gathered to spill some drops of wine as we name them, to show how any suffering—even that of atrocious ancestors— removes some of the joy from our cup. The practice links contemporary injustices and historic harm, inviting guests to name the atrocities we yet see, in the hopes that we will take a different path forward than those ancient oppressors.

As we make sense of our atrocious ancestors, may we seek out the true stories, may we confront and hold our ancestors accountable, and may we seek a way to be accountable to those they harmed, as we continue our journey with all of the ancestors.

Where We Can Go From Here

○ *If you want to write and reflect on this chapter's theme in your own life:*

Take on that question provided by Cisa Payuyo in the chapter. Think about an ancestor you need to tell, "You did [this thing] wrong." And tell them what you're doing to fix their mess.

○ *If you want to engage a personal ritual around this chapter's theme:*

The purpose of connecting with atrocious ancestors isn't necessarily to erase them, so a ritual like cord-cutting might not work. But think of an ancestor who caused harm. Hold them in your mind's eye (or if you have a photo, look at it) and send them the message, "I wish you peace. I wish that you would create peace." We can invite them to do better and be better as an ancestor than they were on this plane. This exercise may allow some of our own pain or frustration to shift as well.

○ *If you want to engage your activist or spiritual group in a practice that will help them begin to connect with ancestors in new ways as part of their work to dismantle white supremacy:*

Share with each other a story of an atrocious ancestor. When each person finishes sharing, have the group look at the person and say, "You are not your ancestors' worst actions." You may also notice overlap and similarities, and what that is calling you all toward collectively, which you can discuss after everyone has shared and everyone has received the words of absolution.

Chapter Four

Ancestors who break our hearts

*Our ancestors are totally essential to our every waking moment,
although most of us don't even have the faintest idea about their
lives, their trials, their hardships or challenges.*
—Annie Lennox

Many of the stories of ancestors, especially the heartbreaking stories,
are told as a story imparting values or morals. My family tells the story
of my great-grandmother, whom I have seen in photos, head shaved and
dressed in the white sari of a widow, eyes clouded over with glaucoma.
The family story is that she was widowed young, and her son was
supposed to inherit the land; another person in the village, wanting
the land for himself, poisoned her son, and out of her mother-love and
heartache, she cried herself blind.

The lesson our family takes from this story is that nothing is purer
or more real than a mother's love. But the story could also be about
patriarchy. My great-grandmother had no claim to the land as a
woman, which left her in a precarious situation in life. Or the story
could have been about lack of medical access. Glaucoma was treatable
even then in places outside the village. Sometimes the moral of a
heartbreaking family story tells us a great deal about the family
ethos. It is OK, even good, to re-examine those stories and let our

hearts break all over again in different ways as we look at them with different frameworks. In grieving with and for them, we might also learn about ourselves and even about what we're being called to do and be in the world today.

The summer after my father passed away, my mother and I spent a month on the island of Great Cumbrae in western Scotland where her gran and her mum had grown up, and where she spent all her summers until she moved to England. For some reason, while I was there, I came to learn about the Highland Clearances, a controversial period in Scotland's history when certain inhabitants were forced off of their lands, and the clan system began to unravel. For generations, the heads of clans had been responsible for the survival and well-being of the members, but beginning in the 1750s, clan chiefs, perhaps influenced by the English lords' very different relationship to land ownership, began pushing family members off the land. The relationship between clan and land was severed. The relationship between land and power and money replaced it.

During our visit, I took a foraging tour of Great Cumbrae led by a man who had left his job in a molecular science lab to pursue a deepening understanding of his ancestors' natural medicine. This was his first tour specifically of Great Cumbrae, the place where he, like my mother, had spent all of his summers growing up. He showed us which flowers we could turn into tinctures, which leaves and flowers and pods made for delicious salads, and most interestingly he pointed out fireweed. Fireweed grows wild, originates in Russia, and makes a nutrient-rich tea. When the East India Trading Company determined it needed to turn a profit, it rejected the local fireweed that had been the most popular tea in Britain (and possibly just as healthy) and launched a rigorous advertising campaign touting the value of Indian tea and its superiority. This created a huge cultural shift and helped to further devalue our ancestors' relationship to their land.

On the same tour he also took our tour group to the beach and let us try the roots of a water plant that our ancestors had used as a starch before potatoes were imported. As the bravest of us munched on the roots and squinched up our faces, someone asked him, "Do you *like* this?"

He responded, "It reminds me of the innovation of my ancestors that allowed us to survive for so long in such mean conditions." In other words, NO, he did *not* like those roots. Potatoes are delicious. We all know that.[25]

Not long after that tour, my mother and I visited the People's Story Museum in Edinburgh. One display case held some of the same foods we had eaten on that tour, and the description noted that "our people used to eat kale and seaweed."

In the typical Scottish diet today, potatoes and peas are the standard vegetables, even at good restaurants. It is well known that Scottish lifespans are ten years shorter than English lifespans, and my mother likes to joke that it's because Scottish sugar intake is about ten pounds more per year than the English. That is true, but I found myself pondering in part the cultural supremacy that disrupted a sparse but healthier diet than the one the English gave them. (Although fish and chips . . . I'll keep that. The Scots have really mastered fried foods. They have taken the offerings of the colonizers and perfected them. I even had deep fried battered pizza slices on that trip, which . . . at some point you're just showing off, I think.)

One day my mother and I were walking up to the golf club at the top of the island. (I know what you're thinking, but the town of Millport on Great Cumbrae was always the working man's holiday spot. Remember who invented golf and remember that this golf course was built by people who worked for a living. The town was, after all, named for its port and its mill.) As we huffed our way up the hill, I pointed out a couple of pretty farmhouses on working farms.

"Yeah, they've let them get a bit scruffy," my mother commented. "Used to take a bit more pride in them."

We went into the clubhouse, had some very bad tea (no fireweed, just Lipton with water that wasn't quite hot enough), and a Mars bar. Before we took them outside to enjoy the view, we started chatting with the barman about the changes to the island. My mother pointed out my third cousin's name on some of the tournament plaques from back in the day. We all talked about the one or two years missing from the plaques because all the men were at war. (There are two memorials on

---

[25]As of the printing of this book, Michael is still offering foraging tours in and around Glasgow and nearby towns and islands such as Great Cumbrae. You can find him on Facebook at Tenement Forager, which is such a glorious ancestor-honoring name.

the island—one for all the men who served and one for the women and men who never returned.) Then we asked about the farms adjacent to the golf course. "Oh, aye. My girlfriend grew up in the one right before the course," he said. "But then the Marquess of Bute (who owned our neighboring island as well as Great Cumbrae) sold them off. Now it's all tenant farmers." When we went outside, I said, "Makes sense why they're so scruffy, huh?"

Now, the Highland Clearances, where the clan chiefs stopped guaranteeing that anyone from the clan could lease land in clan territory was over two hundred years before the Marquess of Bute sold off the land in Millport. But the choices of ancestors in power to become commercial landlords instead of leaders of their clans had ripple effects lasting generations. So, by the time the Marquess of Bute fell on hard times, he had no problem selling off land. In doing so, he disregarded the connections between so many people, as if his ancestors hadn't worked that land with the ancestors of the people working the land today.

The choices made back in the 1700s had changed the very nature of the island over time, much as it had the whole country. The relationship of the people to the land had been broken. And my heart broke with it as I thought about all of these layered costs of disinvestment, of cultural supremacy, of an extraction mentality infecting the minds and hearts of the landowners. No wonder life expectancies were lower. No wonder diets were worse. No wonder addiction rates were higher.

My "sister from another mister," Yvonne, is one of my favorite anti-racism co-training colleagues. On a recent visit to Alabama to lead a workshop, her plane landed early enough that she was able to take a brief visit to the Equal Justice Initiative's Legacy Museum. Best known for its nearby National Lynching Memorial, the Museum was established by Bryan Stevenson as a way of helping this nation tell the hardest parts of its story, while also giving people a chance to grieve. Until we tell that story, until we grieve, until we have a moral reckoning—confronting this legacy and working to do right by the innumerable martyred ancestors—this ugly part of our nation's history will continue to misshape us.

A few months before this trip, Yvonne's great-aunt had passed away. Only three of ten children in her generation were still alive. At the repast after the funeral, another of Yvonne's great-aunts pulled her aside and whispered to her, "There are things I need to tell you since there are so few of us left. My mother, your great-grandmother, had a secret. She was white." It was a secret she had taken to her grave with her.

It seemed to Yvonne a strange secret to have kept. Yvonne is proud to be Black, but she would not have loved her great-grandmother less for being white. She didn't see how anyone in the family would have cared or even been shocked, although people had always understood her simply to be light-skinned. She didn't understand why it had been kept a secret for thirty years.

When Yvonne went to the museum maybe two months after her great-aunt's funeral, she came across an exhibit about the legal punishments, cultural costs and risks of violence faced by mixed-race couples. It clicked with Yvonne as she viewed the exhibit: it was illegal for her great-grandmother to be both white and in love with Yvonne's great-grandfather, a Black man. It was illegal and potentially fatal. In that pain of solidarity and love, Yvonne encountered her great-grandmother in a new way.

Stories about Black people passing for white in order to survive have become increasingly common. A recent Netflix movie, *Passing*, is about sisters who could both pass as white but took very different paths in life, with one suffering the constant microaggressions of a racist husband and society and the other suffering racism but still staying grounded in her heritage and family. I have a deep personal interest in the costs of passing as someone who often can do so myself. Because I had a family committed to encouraging me to embrace all of who I am, my heart does break for the ancestors who did not get that choice. While I also recognize all the overwhelming privilege that comes with my light skin, and accompanied theirs, too, it is a terrible burden to carry secrets, to hide a part of yourself away.[26]

Sometimes the heart-breaking stories of ancestral pain are lesser known but devastating in their historical proximity and in the audacity of the oppressors. You may have had the chance to see the 2002 movie *Rabbit Proof Fence*, based on the true story of three Aboriginal girls who ran away from a residential school in Australia in the 1930s. The schools were part of a government program that intended to eventually marry "half-caste" youth to working-class white men in a practice of

---

[26]For an excellent reflection on the history of literature regarding passing in a Black-White context, please read https://www.topic.com/passing-in-moments

cultural genocide. The end goal was to so dilute the "Aboriginal blood," eradicating the population through intermarriage.[27]

The United States and Canada engaged in an identical practice with church-run residential schools on Native reservations, my friend Dave pointed out to me. Dave lives on the reservation of the federated Yakama Nation. He also played a key role in closing our denomination's formal ministry to the Yakama people in 2015. He now runs a farm and program where faith communities send delegations to work on the farm and learn about racial justice and eco-justice. Dave is a white man with a deep dedication to helping other white and non-Indigenous people to first understand the Doctrine of Discovery and then to repudiate it in the hope of mending harm. The Doctrine of Discovery was first articulated by a pope in the fifteenth century and became a part of the United States legal system through a nineteenth-century Supreme Court Case.[28] It is the principle in international law that the country which "discovers" a land subsequently owns it. The obvious problem with that lies in its failure to recognize the existing inhabitants of a land as worthy of owning it, or even acknowledging their humanity.

During his introductory workshop, Dave talks about an intern who once spent the summer at the farm. She looked white, had curly red hair, and seemingly had a deeper tie to her college than the reservation. By the end of the summer, however, she realized that her grandmother had once lived on the Yakama reservation. Due to the ways the missionaries had "helped" her grandmother marry into whiteness, over the generations, the family came to see themselves as white and forgot their Indigenous roots. This young woman, Dave noted in that first workshop, embodied the Doctrine of Discovery and its attempt at cultural erasure.

We need to grieve things from the chapters on embarrassing ancestors and atrocious ancestors, as well as these ancestors whose suffering

---

[27]I was fortunate enough to be in Australia when their government officially repented of that horrific sin of forced removal and assimilation of Aboriginal peoples, with overwhelming support of the Australian people for that act. The apology came in 2008 after work emerging from a formal report in 1995 after a federal inquiry. https://www.nma.gov.au/defining-moments/resources/national-apology

[28]If the Doctrine of Discovery is a new term to you, a helpful starting place to understand this tool of white supremacy that was then institutionalized in order to dehumanize Indigenous people in order to justify the theft of their land is https://upstanderproject.org/firstlight/doctrine

breaks our hearts. I use that phrase on purpose—*breaking our hearts.* It aligns with the particular community organizing methodology I use and believe in, Faith-Rooted Organizing, which was formalized by James Lawson and Alexia Salvatierra and was shaped by the Gandhian spiritual struggle for independence from British rule, the US Freedom Movement (sometimes called the Civil Rights Movement), the Latin American Liberation Theology movement, and the Theology of Struggle in the Philippines. This faith-rooted community organizing differs from traditional community organizing in that traditional community organizing usually galvanizes around the question, "What's pissing you off?" But faith-rooted organizing galvanizes around "What is breaking your heart?" There are other variations—*what's breaking God's heart or the heart of the universe? What is out of balance or alignment?* But it speaks to me.

In naming what is breaking our hearts, we can get clarity on what our work needs to be. We also get clarity on the ways in which we need to engage that work. Whether we are called fierce, compassionate, or accountable, we know we will need a range of tools. We know, from the great Audre Lorde, that "the master's tools will never dismantle the master's house."[29]

That house—of erasure, of eradication, of oppression, and pain—was presumably built generations ago. Our ancestors may have been forced to build it, work on the land surrounding it, or may have lived in it. In light of those varied possibilities, how do we go about dismantling it? With whom should we partner in the work? How will we go about dismantling what has been in ways that are accountable to the ancestors harmed in its construction?

In future chapters, we will also ask how might we connect with ancestors' wisdom to determine what to build instead.

As we sit with these ancestors who break our hearts, we might need to forgive some of them. We may need to cry alongside them. We may need to promise them we will do right by them. We may need to lament with ancestors who made choices with painful repercussions, seeing those as the best choice they had.

---

[29]Originally the title of Lorde's comments at a 1979 panel on "The Personal and the Political" at the Second Sex conference, it is also published in Crossing Press's 1984 collection of her essays entitled "Sister Outsider."

In one of the wisdom circles that shaped this book, my friend Cathy said that some of their work with their ancestors was to be aware that their ancestors had developed a stoicism and emotional distance over generations that they were sure was intended to keep those ancestors and their descendants safe. Still, Cathy also needed to grieve what that emotional distance and stoicism had cost Cathy in terms of family relations, and to grieve, too, what it had cost their ancestors and descendants. They said, "I have to ask myself also, what has the 'frozen chosen' culture withheld from me even as I know that culture served their safety?"

Like Cathy, we may need to dig deeper—beyond the frozen crust of our ancestors' worlds—to see what has been withheld from us, preventing us from fully grieving harmful realities, and healing for the future.

My colleague, Stacey Park-Milbern, a well-regarded disability justice activist, wrote an essay on disabled ancestors and how they shape us for the movement not long before her death in 2020. The following is an excerpt from that essay.

> Ancestorship, like love, is expansive and breaks manmade boundaries cast upon it, like the nuclear family model or artificial nation-state borders. My ancestors are disabled people who lived looking out of institution windows wanting so much more for themselves. It's because of them that I know that, in reflecting on what is a "good" life, an opportunity to contribute is as important as receiving supports one needs. My ancestors are people torn apart from loves by war and displacement. It's because of them I know the power of building home with whatever you have, wherever you are, whomever you are with. My ancestors are queers who lived in the American South. It's because of them I understand the importance of relationships, place and living life big, even if it is dangerous. All of my ancestors know longing. Longing is often our connecting place.[30]

Note the theme of longing and ancestors as we wrap up this chapter on ancestors who break our hearts . . . and possibly break our hearts open.

In the spring of 2021, I received a small fellowship from RADAR Productions as part of their ongoing work to connect queer artists of

---

[30]https://disabilityvisibilityproject.com/2019/03/10/on-the-ancestral-plane-crip-hand-me-downs-and-the-legacy-of-our-movements/

color with the LGBTQ+ Archives at the San Francisco Public Library. Their archivist connected me with resources in my subject area, and I got to share an art piece a month later.

I set out to create a visually accompanied audio essay about queer South Asian immigrant ancestors in the US. Mason, the archivist, and I met by Zoom, and they gave me great information, listened to what my project was about so they could supply me with the right materials, and then they said, "also, I am going to do a tarot reading from the ancestors for you." I'm not big into tarot, but hey—free reading.

As they pulled the cards, Mason told me, "The ancestors are saying what you're delving into could cause you real pain and depression, so they are encouraging you to seek out and tell stories not just of trauma but of fierceness, resilience, and joy."

These words of ancestral advice are wise. As any activist or pastor knows, you need joy and hope to balance out the deep pain that can come from loving and struggling alongside others.

Below is an excerpt from my essay about ancestors that broke my heart open, written April 2021. While it is very particular to me, I hope you encounter your own longings for your ancestors.

> I've been chasing a longing for a while now. It's maybe captured by the tattoo I gifted myself for my 45th birthday [a replica of a painting of queer South Asian lovers by the Caribbean South Asian artist Shalini Seereeram]. I'm not sure I had a name for the longing, but it's beginning to emerge . . . a longing for the before. A longing for people who can help me make sense of the what is now . . . a longing for a path to how to navigate my five-years-new identity as queer in addition to mixed race, mixed religion South Asian immigrant.
>
> The documentary "Khush" (ecstatic pleasure in Urdu), a documentary about the gay and lesbian community in India in the 1980s asked a community member what he liked about khush, about being gay: "What do I like about being gay? The sex, and the solidarity: the brotherhood, the sisterhood."
>
> One of the first same-gender loving publications for South Asians, Shamakami, sought to reclaim an ancient Bengali word that means "love for an equal" or "love for the same," a

term sometimes used for women who desire women, and I'll be honest, I thrill at these new-to-me names I want to try on like I try on saris to the delight of my family in India and the discomfort of people in my neighborhood in Oakland. And at the same time, I'm a person of three soils, not fluent in any of them culturally and less so as a queer person. Which are my clothes to claim? Which are my words to claim? How big can my identity go? What am I allowed to long for and what longing is born of ignorance?

What does it mean to live between and across cultures?

South Asians have hung out on this land of Indigenous Californians for well over a century, including queer South Asians. We know many of them from early in the last century ironically because of their criminal histories, records kept by the prisons and courts. My friend Anirvan Chatterjee has collected some of their images into a zine, inspired in part by the research of Nayan Shah in his book *Stranger Intimacy.* Some of their stories are shocking, and some of their stories are heartbreaking. Some of the men here are listed for "crimes against nature" because in the 1910s and 1920s, a narrative began to emerge in white society that sex between men was an infiltrating perversion inflicted on otherwise good white American men by not American not-quite-men from Asia and particularly India.

One case I can't stop thinking about is Keshn Singh and Jack Lynch in Stockton in 1928, one of the earliest trials for the sin of same sex oral sex. Singh, who had lived in the US since the age of four, was cast in the courtroom as the degenerate foreigner, corrupting good wholesome Americans, sent to San Quentin for four years to protect America from him corrupting other men "by furnishing himself as a subject to be acted upon." Since the ancestors asked me to focus on stories of strength and resilience and joy and not on shame, I come back to the theme of longing. Of Keshn Singh and Jamil Singh and Rola Singh and their longing for touch, for companionship, for khush. Strong, rugged, working class men who were mostly on people's radars because they paired up with white men and were therefore a different kind of threat . . . what does it mean for these men to be my ancestors of choice, my siblings in longing?

Colonialism erased queerness from the histories of the Mughal emperors and the lines of the Urdu poets, leaving a heterosexual God from Muslim Desis to call on. The fingerprints of colonialism also mar a complex relationship between Hinduism and its multiplicity of understandings of queer and genderqueer and trans stories that date back thousands of years. Colonialism reshaped Hinduism from complexity to simplicity, leaving the stories untouched but some buried and others rendered purely metaphorical or for the gods but not for us so that the gender bending and queer stories of the sacred texts are not allowed to be tools of empowerment. So, which gods were we allowed to bring with us? Do we get to invite different gods to join us here now when they are from so far away?

This winter I heard someone say, "I have realized I equate my queerness with longing," and it broke my heart. It felt so incomplete. It felt connected to centuries of repression and oppression. And yet longing is so real and human. In some ways I see a thread of longing throughout this rich story of my ancestors of choice. I see it in the art of queer Pakistani American artist Salman Toor. I see it in the hidden stories of Punjabi farm workers locked up for crimes against nature. I see it in the founders of Shamakami seeking love between equals or love between same. I see it in the love between the characters in the film *Fire,* whose story awakened so much in so many of us. I see it in my family of choice whose saris tie end to end reaching back to a land 8,000 miles away, nine yards at a time. And at its culmination, I see longing being met through integration of self.

At its heart, maybe the longing is a gift because it moves me towards connection. Maybe it connects me to ancestors and to lovers and to community. Maybe I don't need to be afraid of longing, because it is ultimately what connects me and you.[31]

---

[31]Which can be viewed here: https://youtu.be/ddc5Kh-3nRw

Where We Can Go From Here:

○ *If you want to write and reflect on this chapter's theme in your own life:*

Is there a major social or economic event that affected your family negatively (like the Highland Clearances)? Take some time to connect a heartbreaking story from your family's narrative to the larger social forces that contributed to it.

○ *If you want to engage a personal ritual around this chapter's theme:*

Think of an ancestor who suffered. If you have an image that represents them, hold onto it and share with them that you know they struggled, and share what you're doing to make things better for people dealing with similar things today. Send love and be open to receiving love in return.

○ *If you want to engage your activist or spiritual group in a practice that will help them begin to connect with ancestors in new ways as part of their work to dismantle white supremacy:*

Share a story of an ancestor whose story breaks your heart. Invite the group to share what they heard, and what words of consolation or encouragement they'd offer that person now. End by naming how you're creating a better world for those ancestors' descendants.

Chapter Five

Inheriting Ancestral Trauma

To be alive at all is to have scars.
—John Steinbeck, Winter of our Discontent

Note from the Author:
I am not an expert on the subject of epigenetics, the science of
intergenerational trauma. There is some high-level science and
psychiatry in the mix of this subject. To delve into it more fully,
please read My Grandmother's Hands *by Resmaa Menakem, who*
does brilliant work on this subject (although he states up front
that he focuses primarily on the present, and he focuses mainly
on Black and white people, so it will require interpretation,
inference, and translation for those of us from other cultures).
But I want to spend some time on the subject because what we've
learned about the epigenetics of generational trauma since the
mid-2010s, and the healing modalities people have developed to
reconcile and shift that trauma, is remarkable.

When I was a child and doing something like beating eggs, if my arm got tired and I started stirring counterclockwise, my mother would freak out. "*Stirring counterclockwise means you're a witch!*" she would yell. I would laugh, even though she was serious.

In researching this book, I read a blog post on Saining, the Scottish-Celtic parallel to smudging done in some Indigenous practices. What I liked most was that the article was written to encourage non-Indigenous people not to misappropriate Indigenous rituals. The author offered this essay for people of Scottish descent and hoped non-Scots would find their cultural equivalents.

I read the essay with vague interest as it explained why the practices were syncretic (adopting some Christian elements was what allowed the ancient practices to survive), how it wasn't for general cleansing but for revealing overlooked spirits and sending out troubling ones, and what types of kindling were used. But then my eye caught on the ritual midwives would use, where the smoke (from a tree with young sap, causing black smoke) was waved in a sunwise pattern, the prosperous direction—"deosil" in Gaelic—that is, clockwise. (In low Scots, counterclockwise is "widdershins," which is so evocative of the way *not* to do something, isn't it? The Gaelic is "tuathal," proving that lowland Scots are way more fun than highlanders.)

In the monthly white people's wisdom circle of 2021 that contributed to the shaping of this book, we spent a chunk of time on witches because there is little understanding of where the fear of witches came from and because so many people in the group had connections to that story of how witch hunting had caused damage in their family lines. Many of us tied that fear and recrimination around witches to concerns about threats to politics and power far more than any threat to religion or faith. As one participant whose family remains largely conservative Christian with a low tolerance for women's leadership put it, "The burning times never ended."

In *Caliban and the Witch: Women, the Body and Primitive Accumulation,* Silvia Federici points to how serf uprisings in Europe and North Africa preceded mass efforts to demonize and round up "witches" as an effort to destabilize those movements for land justice. Ultimately, Federici argues, capitalism was established as a counter-reform because by the Middle Ages, "the revolt of the peasantry against the landlords had become endemic, massified, and frequently armed."[32] Control of women's bodies and women's labor was part of the strategy of landlords, which naturally led to an attack against magic since women were the ones most likely to be called on for healing and other practices to address things beyond villagers' control.

---

[32]Federici, Silvia. *Caliban and the Witch: Women, the Body and Primitive Accumulation,* 25.

For their claim to magical power undermined the power of the authorities and the state, giving confidence to the poor in their ability to manipulate the natural and social environment and possibly subvert the constituted order. It is doubtful, on the other hand, that the magical arts that women had practiced for generations would have been magnified into a demonic conspiracy had they not occurred against a background of an intense social crisis and struggle.[33]

Federici writes about the disempowerment of women, poor people, and Jewish people (there were often anti-Semitic elements to anti-witch campaigns) and also an intentional turning away from ancestral wisdom and healing practices all wrapped up in this period that ultimately led to capitalism and "the Enlightenment," which, along with some excellent scientific discoveries, resulted in the rejection of non-European wisdom and in the violent pseudo-science of race.

So, what does it mean to be descended from the women who were burned (or more often hung)? What does it mean spiritually? What does it mean for our self-understanding and our understanding of the world? Finally, what does it mean biologically?

> So, what does it mean to be descended from the women who were burned (or more often hung)?

I was one of many people deeply moved by the 2015 scientific study that found that the *expression* of DNA of Holocaust survivors was altered for three generations. It made intuitive sense to so many of us—our aversions, our fears. They made sense in this context of us carrying the trauma of the generations before us.[34]

It turns out, and the lead scientist has been clear, that those results were from a sample size too small to be used as formal verification of a pattern, but they were, he insisted, a valuable beginning.

Two years prior, in 2013, a study of mice showed that if a mouse was trained to associate the scent of cherry blossom with trauma, the next two generations would have a marker tagged onto their DNA that made them sensitive to the scent of cherry blossom. They wouldn't have a

---

[33]Ibid., 704.
[34]https://www.bbc.com/future/article/20190326-what-is-epigenetics

trauma response, but they would have a sensitivity to that scent relative to other mice.[35] That's epigenetics, the little markers added to our DNA based on previous generations' trauma. Our DNA doesn't change, but little tags get added or taken away, almost little on-off switches in case we need them. Research on both animals and people has shown that Post-Traumatic Stress Disorder (PTSD) can lead to changes in RNA as well, leading to increased eating, response to insulin, and risk-taking behavior in the next two generations. And the research is only beginning. Right now, it focuses exclusively on the sperm because "eggs are so much harder to study."[36]

When Brent Bezo lived in Ukraine in the 1990s, he noticed his behavior beginning to change. He wondered at first if the change was related to adopting local cultural practices, but as a social scientist chose to explore the question more rigorously—what *was* local culture and what had created it? He had heard many people speak of Holodomor, the mass starvation of millions of Ukrainians during what many believed was an intentionally attempted genocide during the Stalin regime.

As Bezo interviewed survivors, their children and grandchildren, they named behaviors reminiscent of those of the RNA research about intergenerational trauma: "Risky health behaviors, anxiety and shame, food hoarding, overeating, authoritarian parenting styles, high emotional neediness on the part of parents and low community trust and cohesiveness—what many described as living in 'survival mode.'"[37]

In an article on that research, Bezo reported that "each generation seemed to kind of learn from the previous one, with survivors telling children, 'Don't trust others, don't trust the world.'"

> [As of 2019, Bezo] was conducting a larger quantitative study to compare intergenerational effects among Ukrainians who remained in the country after the Holodomor, those who emigrated, and a group of Ukrainians unaffected by the event. The work is part of an emerging line of research and clinical work in psychology and related disciplines that is exploring whether and how mass cultural and historical traumas affect future generations. Bezo's observations are compatible with

---

[35]https://www.bbc.com/future/article/20190326-what-is-epigenetics
[36]Eyeroll.
[37] https://www.apa.org/monitor/2019/02/legacy-trauma

those of researchers exploring the intergenerational effects of the Holocaust, the Khmer Rouge killings in Cambodia, the Rwandan genocide, the displacement of American Indians, and the enslavement of African Americans. The transgenerational effects are not only psychological but familial, social, cultural, neurobiological, and possibly even genetic as well, the researchers say.[38]

Most of the people I know who are drawn to this subject, like myself, are particularly interested in epigenetics. What I appreciated about the Bezo article, however, is that even if there were no DNA markers or no RNA changes, we carry the imprint of ancestral trauma through the lessons our family internalizes and passes on through generations, as well the narratives we internalize over generations about how to stay safe. There are ways we are shaped by others' fears until they become our own fears.

These responses, rippling through generations, are known as "adaptive styles." The Danieli Inventory on Multigenerational Trauma was developed by those researching the adaptive styles of survivors of the Holocaust in Nazi Germany. Four adaptive styles emerged from the survivors' responses—"victim," "numb," "fighter" and "those who made it." In her research, Yael Danieli noticed things like a high need for control and a deep sense of protectiveness of parents among the children of holocaust survivors as well as immature dependency.

She called these reactions "reparative adaptational impacts" to highlight the notion that survivors' progeny use them to try to repair the world for their parents, their grandparents, and themselves—largely unconsciously. Her related theory predicts a pathway between the initial trauma, the family's history and post-trauma sociocultural milieu, the adaptational styles of survivors, and the intensity of their children's and grandchildren's reparative reactions to them.[39]

Research found high rates of generalized anxiety disorder, major depressive episodes, and PTSD. These rates varied considerably based on whether they had high or low reparative adaptational impact scores and depending on which of the four adaptive styles their parents inhabited (victim, numb, fighter, and "those who made it").

---

[38]IBID.
[39] *American Journal of Orthopsychiatry*, Vol. 86, No. 6, 2016, 639–651.

Similar research among the descendants of Indigenous people who survived the 1950s relocation policies in Canada reveals similar results. That research is important because according to the authors of "The Intergenerational Effects of Relocation Policies on Indigenous Families,"

> Government relocation policy of the 1950s provides a somewhat recent example of an acculturation policy. It affected a cohort of whom many still survive and affords the opportunity to measure the psychosocial impact of moving individuals from reservations to urban employment settings.[40]

What's important to note is that research shows that while trauma was passed down, so was the method of navigating that trauma. Every parent I know these days is trying to find ways to pass on different patterns to their children than they received from parents with fewer tools, so this may not be surprising to you. Because there is so much current interest in epigenetics and its role in inherited trauma, I want to pause and note that social scientists who study more than just the biology (and I am confident this is true of pure biologists and neuroscientists as well) point out that things like DNA and RNA are only part of how generational inheritance plays itself out.

> Generational ties are particularly valued because elders are viewed as repositories of cultural knowledge, spirituality, and traditional language. Their life experience is enormously respected, and they are turned to for direction and advice. When these linkages are disturbed the consequences ripple through subsequent generations.[41]

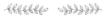

Back in 2018, I got to be part of an event a colleague coordinated to help her network of volunteers learn more about Indigenous justice issues. The keynote speaker was 2020 Presidential candidate and Indigenous rights activist Mark Charles. Among his many compelling points (including a proposal for a Truth Commission on Indigenous Justice), Charles made reference to the powerful book *Post-Traumatic*

[40]https://www.apa.org/monitor/2019/02/legacy-trauma
[41]https://www.yesmagazine.org/opinion/2018/06/18/indian-country-remembers-the-trauma-of-children-taken-from-their-parents

Slave Syndrome, which talks about inherited trauma among African Americans. Charles continued, however, to note that we also need to discuss "Post-Traumatic Slaveholder Syndrome." While my notes from his talk have been lost, I recall he said that white people are just as likely to carry an unstudied, unexamined epigenetic inheritance of those enslaving days. Charles seemed to imply, or at least I was inferring, that yet again, science was focusing on the symptom rather than the root cause, ensuring that the actual disease of white supremacy could continue to survive.

The reason I remember this part of his presentation so well is what he demanded from people of color in response to that reality. He said that too often our response to this Post-Traumatic Slaveholder Syndrome in white people is to tiptoe around it for fear of setting it off or to confront it aggressively because we're so tired of it. If our goal was to change things rather than survive it or be right about it, we need to learn from how professionals treat people with trauma. They don't poke it antagonistically and without a goal in mind because that shuts someone down. They don't tiptoe around it either, because that leaves the trauma in place where it continues to cause harm. A good therapist figures out where the trigger point is and compassionately says, "OK, we're going to stay here for a little while."

While he invited people of color to do that work, on the day I heard him speak, he was well aware of his majority-white audience. (Mark Charles is a smart man.) Although he was speaking to the people of color during that portion of his talk, he indirectly introduced to the white people in the room that this was actually *their* work to do, reminding them that people of color currently have to walk around them like they are landmines set to go off, and that will likely continue to be the case until white people begin to investigate what it means to carry around that very different version of ancestral trauma.

In his incredibly practical book grounded in body practices and healing pathways for Black people and white people, Resmaa Menakem writes about what happens to the descendants of people who participated in horrors. His focus is on how trauma shows up in our bodies, and he also recognizes the shift from the biological to the communitarian. In other words, while recent coverage of generational trauma has focused on epigenetics, perhaps an even more significant way generational trauma shapes all of us is collectively, culturally, whether our ancestors suffered the trauma, perpetuated it, or remained unengaged or unaware. In describing a photo of a lynching from 1920, he makes this point:

> What happened to the men in the lynching photo—and to many, many other men and women like them—was deep and persistent trauma. This trauma got transmitted and compounded through multiple generations; eventually, it began to look like culture.[42]

The way I understand culture is that it's about rituals, worldviews, and ways of life. Whether we carry trauma in our DNA or not, we carry it in our culture, and if we are propping up the dominant culture, then we carry it in our culture's resistance to dealing with that trauma.

I recently came across the work of Tada Hozumi, a Japanese Canadian spiritual healer. He wrote an essay on healing the ancestral trauma of whiteness. While I highly recommend reading the whole essay,[43] here is a short portion explaining whiteness (which affects all of us on this land across races, although in different ways).

> My observation is that whiteness is born out of cultural complex trauma, the wounds of being disconnected from ancestry.
>
> In regular trauma psychotherapy it is understood that one of the greatest factors that determine our ability to regulate our nervous system and handle traumatic stress is the quality of our 'attachment': our imprinted feelings of safety or unsafety in our relationships to our caregivers.
>
> Conceptualizing a cultural nervous system means extending this idea of attachment to not just caregivers in our childhood but to what we may call our parental cultures. The cultural soma's ability to handle traumatic stress is deeply impacted by its attachment to its parental cultures.
>
> And of course, anything that affects the cultural soma has an impact on our individual somas. This is how whiteness works.

Soma is the Greek word for body. Somatic practice, the practice of connecting our bodies' reactions to the reactions of our hearts and

---

[42]Menakem, Resmaa. *My Grandmother's Hands.* P. 203.

[43]https://web.archive.org/web/20210319034220/https://selfishactivist.com/what-it-means-to-heal-white-supremacy/

minds, is an increasingly popular tool in social justice movements. Hozumi may mean here "our collective body" when she says, "cultural soma," or she may mean the almost physical response of our collective culture to the situation we find ourselves in. If you know what the phrase "breathing a collective sigh of relief" feels like, you've witnessed a somatic body response to a collective experience.

How has our cultural soma in the United States been shaped by our ancestors' varied adaptive responses to trauma?

In my work and in my life, I spend a lot of time thinking about accountability. How can we be responsible and hold others responsible for the harm and the good we or they cause?

In one of the wisdom circles comprised of people of color, I asked whether anyone in the circle thinks in terms of accountability to our ancestors who suffered unspeakable harms. My friend Tai Amri took it to another level of accountability. He said:

> I like that word *accountability*—I wish I didn't have oppressive ancestry; part of the accountability is healing my lineage, the known (an ancestor who was abusive and alcoholic), and the unknown. The Ifa tradition means you still work with those ancestors so we can do work they weren't able to do; they can help us to course correct and not make those same mistakes. I have Quaker ancestors, and so many of the [Indigenous] "boarding schools" were run by Quakers. I need to know all I can and tell those stories, especially in Quaker circles.[44]

Whether we know exactly who our ancestors were or not, we know we are shaped by the repercussions of a traumatic history. That gives us a chance to examine ourselves, give ourselves self-compassion that can radiate back to ancestors still hurting, and do the work to free ourselves from the harm our ancestors did by doing something different.

If we believe ancestral trauma is real, biologically or in how we are enculturated or both, and if we look into our history and believe we are marked with the repercussions of that trauma, what is the resilience work we can do to create healing for those who come after us? Is there

---

[44]I just want to pause and note that if people of color are asking what we can do to address the harm our own ancestors (spiritual, cultural, biological) did, it makes me even more embarrassed for the people who are fighting to suppress the telling of our whole history.

. . . .

If we believe ancestral trauma is real, biologically or in how we are enculturated or both, and if we look into our history and believe we are marked with the repercussions of that trauma, what is the resilience work we can do to create healing for those who come after us? Is there work we should do to release our ancestors and create healing?

work we should do to release our ancestors and create healing?

Conversations in my part of the world about ancestral trauma are fairly common these days. Inspired in part by the activists and organizers with the Ohlone people in the Native American territory known as Oakland, we talk about *ancestral resilience* as well as ancestral trauma. The reason we talk about it is that in the face of horrors, our people survived. They did what they had to, yes, and that itself is painful, but in addition to the horrors that recoded their DNA, they passed on to us tools and skills and stories and spirit to survive horrible things.

My Indigenous spiritual organizer colleague Corrina is part of a movement to preserve some of the Ohlone languages. She notes that part of how her ancestors survived attempted genocide was by replacing their language with Spanish so they could pass as Mexicans and survive. But Spirit whispered to Corrina who she really was so that she could reconnect with the language that was part of her healing.

In the same way that people of color do not want to be known solely for the pain we've experienced due to racism, our ancestors are not only known to us by the trauma they passed on.

My friend Yuki makes the excellent point that in addition to ancestral resilience, we can look to ancestral resistance. There is a growing frustration among people of color at how often nonprofits and foundations talk about investing in the "resilience" of marginalized communities, placing the burden of survival on the marginalized rather than the oppressive force making life so difficult it requires resilience. Moreover, focusing on resilience addresses only the symptom. Yuki says in their work, they lean more toward talking about *resisting*. In one of the people of color wisdom circles I facilitated in 2021, they noted, "It's important to emphasize that resilience is only meaningful when we're working to change the structures that are causing the harm we're resisting." Resisting moves us beyond treating symptoms and into addressing the root cause of the harm.

In the framework of the Storytelling Project Model, we've been noticing the Concealed Stories that the stock story covers up. Part of our own healing might be two-fold: our ancestors passed on to us the trauma of the concealed stories, to protect us from fully trusting the stock stories. Perhaps when it wasn't safe to tell us the stories, the epigenetics passed the story down to keep us alert to the dangers around us. Alive and carrying generational trauma is still alive. Alive and harmed offers some possibility. Dead offers no such hope.

Some of the critique of that term "resilience" is simply this truth: we shouldn't have to be resilient. We have to be resilient because systems are unjust. The systems should instead change. Yet in this in-between world, as we seek to dismantle oppression but while oppression persists, resilience is a gift of ancestors.

Our work is somehow to do both, stay resilient and also resist the systems and structures that caused us this harm in the first place. Perhaps learning the resistance stories of ancestors gives us the courage to do that work for the sake of their healing as well as our own.

This becomes so clear in a particular example where people carry an ancestral trauma, and the trauma has not remained solely in the past but rather continues today.

There are not a vast number of studies on intergenerational trauma effects in the Black community. Alfiee Breeland-Noble, who directs the AAKOMA (African American Knowledge Optimized for Mindfully Healthy Adolescents) Project at Georgetown University, points to a term she uses called "shared stress" to talk about how it shows up in the present. Shared stress is the sense of having to carry everything for one's community because society-at-large cannot be trusted to do right by your community. A current example, she says, is the dread that many African American parents face in talking with sons about potential police encounters.

> It's traumatizing for parents and it's traumatizing for kids. There is a sense among African Americans and other marginalized people that our stressors are unique to us and not necessarily

shared by people outside our groups. So, we share stories of
our lived experiences that help set the stage for how our loved
ones encounter the world.[45]

In turn, that can lead to a general distrust of others outside the group—
particularly those from historically oppressive groups—along with
in-group insularity, she says.

"The talk" is a palpable example of an ancestral trauma that did not
end in the past. Policing in the United States traces its origins back to
groups hired by enslavers to capture human beings and bring them
back to the people who saw them as property more than as human
beings. To this day, Black parents talk with children about how to stay
safe from the institutional descendants of slave catchers. There's a
famous quote about the past not being dead or even past, which some
people quote glibly as patterns from history repeat themselves over
and over. But this is also part of the reality of ancestral trauma. It is not
always or even very often past. This is why connecting with ancestors
amidst current trauma may offer us a chance to learn how to survive
and perhaps also how to resist.

I mentioned earlier that in the white people's wisdom circle I facilitated
for this book, we spent a fair bit of time talking about witches. We talked
about research we had done, particularly connected with the book
Caliban and the Witch, although there are many books on this subject.
We talked about scholars who explained that in the medieval period,
poor men and women shared common cause in fighting for economic
justice and that the witch hunts had targeted women in specific ways to
break apart the cross-gender solidarity among poor people. We talked
about how many times people in power had used that same strategy of
pitting groups against each other in order to retain power.

In that circle, we also talked about how those ancestors' terror stayed
in us over generations. "We carry the burning times in our bodies," one
participant said, explaining why people need to know more about the
politics behind this history, "but we don't know about those times. We
can't heal that which we can't name."

---

[45]https://www.apa.org/monitor/2019/02/legacy-trauma

The group went on to discuss how unhealed trauma results in us causing trauma to others. An example came up of those invisible threads of history: someone shared how the witch hunts kept poor people poor and less able to fight for economic freedom, particularly by taking away any power women held and by deeming their medicine dangerous. (Women generally provided folk medicine, the only type of medicine most people had access to. The witch trials told their communities that folk medicine, the use of herbs and tonics, was witchcraft, cutting off the only access to health remedies most poor people had.) That poverty carried on across generations. And poverty sometimes led to desperation and crime, or simply to the inability to pay debts to landlords, which landed people in jail or the poor house, and sometimes this would repeat across generations because of the inability to ever eliminate a growing mountain of debt.

Many of the indentured servants in the American colonies were drawn from debtors' prisons in Britain, and the jobs available to them when their indenture ended were often undesirable jobs essential to growing other people's wealth, like being a plantation overseer. One person in our group used this connective narrative to show the witch trials and their success in keeping some of her ancestors in poverty, leading eventually to her more recent ancestors playing the brutal role of overseer in the US era of enslavement.

There is a particularly US-ian desire to start with a clean slate and an ongoing commitment to the myth that to do so is possible, as if we don't carry in our social location, in our sense of self-worth, in our community's valuation of us, and in our very DNA, millennia of ancestors. When my friend Marcia embarked on her lifelong work of addressing white supremacy, she said, "She Who Whispers in My Ear said that I couldn't do this work without ancestors."

In engaging those stories and how they have made us who we are, we might experience some freedom. In their stories being acknowledged, perhaps our ancestors will experience some freedom also.

Recently, in reading an essay by Taylor Amari Little, I was reminded that ancestors can provide a real gift to us in the spaces where our own living biological family cannot be what we need. Little is an activist who specializes in creating healing spaces for people of color and LGBTQ+

Muslims. In that essay,[46] he noted that his own father had been absent and unaccountable in his childhood and youth, and so he cultivated a relationship with his ancestors starting when he was thirteen or fourteen. He quoted Myesha Worthington, a Nganga and Root Doctor, who said, "A lot of times it be the ancestors of a neglectful parent who work overtime." Little continues,

> For a long time, I noticed my Soninke and Fulbe/Fulani Ancestors, from my father's side, would show up for me right away, and when they show up, they show up. Proud warriors, fighters, protectors, no-nonsense-takers. I caught on early, understanding that they, as a collective, were stepping in for family I had lost access to the majority of my life.

As we think about ancestral trauma, it is worth remembering that for some of us, ancestors can offer healing in the midst of much more immediate trauma in our families and in our own bodies.

There's a lovely Facebook page called Latinx Parenting. I've tried to avoid Facebook posts in this book, but they had a post that seemed significant to this theme. The image with the post was a screen capture of a tweet by Xavier Dagba (@xavierdagba) stating, "As you focus on clearing your generational trauma, do not forget to claim your generational strengths. Your ancestors gave you more than just wounds."[47] The post goes on to read:

> So often we forget about the fact that our survival, our presence here today, has a great deal to do with the fierce resilience that our ancestors demonstrated to be able to keep themselves and their children alive.
>
> Anytime I laugh, my ancestors laugh with me.
>
> Anytime I dance, I can feel how my ancestor's bodies moved in song.
>
> Anytime I run, I can almost feel the leather of the huaraches on my feet.

---

[46]http://Blackyouthproject.com/how-learning-to-work-with-my-ancestors-created-a-relationship-of-reciprocity-and-parental-support/
[47]https://www.facebook.com/latinxparenting/posts/1743480012488390

Anytime I sing or speak my truth, I know the vibration in my throat is their instrument in the here and now.

Anytime I hug my children, I can feel the embrace of the long line of my abuelitas hugging me in turn.

Not all of them had access to do some of these things freely and comfortably, we know that. And for the ones that couldn't because of the ways and confines of oppression, I remember I am healing for them too.

But—I choose to amplify this: My well Ancestors have given me the awareness that I carry the blueprint of strength, Inner knowing, joy, love, and resilience in my DNA.

And so do you.

And so do your babies.

And so will theirs.

If you're still struggling to figure out what it looks like to heal our ancestral trauma, I want to close by sharing a story I learned about the descendants of Dred Scott and Roger Taney.

You may have heard of Dred Scott. He was enslaved, and his enslavers brought him and his family with them into a free state. After several months, he filed for citizenship and freedom. Taney was the Supreme Court justice who denied Scott and his wife Harriet citizenship. He maintained that Black people did not have any rights except those white people gave them.

Six generations later, the descendants of Roger Taney wrote a play bringing attention to the story in 2016, reached out to the descendants of Dred Scott to apologize personally, and made a formal apology in 2017. The two families continue to meet around a shared commitment to racial justice. They had even begun plans to put up a statue of Dred Scott facing a statue of Roger Taney in order to force deeper conversation when activists removed the original statue instead as part of a larger global movement to eliminate statues of people who played key roles in enslavement and genocide.[48]

---

[48]https://www.wnycstudios.org/podcasts/radiolabmoreperfect/episodes/american-pendulum-ii-dred-scott. I cannot recommend enough that you listen to this show, on the law and race and apologizing for our ancestors...or not having to.

In a joint lecture at University of Oklahoma College of Law, Charlie Taney, the great-great-grandnephew of Roger Taney, and Lynne Jackson, the great-great-granddaughter of Dred Scott, spoke on the steps required for reconciliation. "Reconciliation has three phases," said Taney, reflecting on their first meeting. "The first step is that the party that's caused the harm, that's injured another party, has to do two things. First, they have to admit to it, to say, 'Yup, we did that.' And then they have to go to the other party, and they have to ask for forgiveness. And then the party that's been injured has to have the mercy to forgive them."[49]

Since their reconciliation, Taney and Jackson have worked closely through the Dred Scott Heritage Foundation, which Jackson founded. At the event, both encouraged people to prioritize personal, individual connections alongside political solutions, saying that even something as simple as inviting acquaintances of another race over for dinner can have major positive consequences.

Taney and Jackson hope their personal stories of reconciliation can encourage others to form partnerships and work against racism in America.

"So, if we're going to fix things, we've got to own up to it, we've got to face it," Taney said. "We can't run away from it, we've got to own it, and then we've got to say, 'OK, now what are we going to do about it?'"[50]

I believe this is the good news of both the science and the soul of ancestral trauma. If we are really lucky or really intentional, we can learn what caused the trauma. We can reach out to others carrying that same trauma. We can learn how our ancestors survived. We can learn how they resisted. Those lessons can then equip us to follow their wisdom or to free ourselves from their actions by choosing a different way of being, as best we are able.

In the process of healing, we may find our way toward dismantling the root cause of that trauma for the healing and liberation of our ancestors or to make right the harm they caused.

---

[49] I want to note that they are not saying people who caused harm or their descendants *deserve* reconciliation; they're just explaining what reconciliation is.

[50] https://www.oudaily.com/news/descendants-of-dred-scott-roger-taney-speak-at-ou-college-of-law/article_6d0718f4-5e84-11ea-9839-ef48d677beb1.html

Where We Can Go From Here

○ *If you want to write and reflect on this chapter's theme in your own life:*

Are there any horrible things you know your ancestors participated in? Is there any of what Mark Charles called "Post Traumatic Slaveholder Syndrome" that you carry with you, or some other way your ancestors participated in oppression, even if they were not at the top of the heap?

Take a moment to think about what it would feel like to engage that history as Judge Taney's descendants did. What media could you use? What would feel cathartic? Who would you want to reach out to in order to do some of the healing of the harm your ancestors caused?

○ *If you want to engage a personal ritual around this chapter's theme:*

Spend some time with ancestors who experienced trauma. Light a candle to honor them and to let them know there is light in the darkness now. Share ways your community is better, safer, more kind than the community they knew. If there are hard things now, ask them for comfort and encouragement, since they have also faced hard times.

○ *If you want to engage your activist or spiritual group in a practice that will help them begin to connect with ancestors in new ways as part of their work to dismantle white supremacy:*

If you are aware of lessons you learned about how to protect yourself from threats that are not likely, talk about how you might stop replicating that cycle with the next generation.

SECTION II: The Gifts of Ancestors

In section two, we get to look at more of the resistance stories of our ancestors. And we get to expand beyond biological ancestors to other ancestors whose gifts we can draw on.

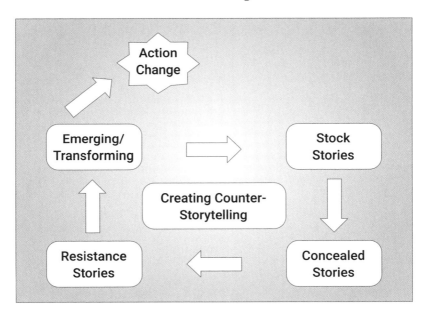

CHAPTER SIX

Cultural Ancestors

In every country and region, there are practices and ways of living and culture that have been handed down from ancestors. Naturally, I feel that these should be respected.

—Shinzo Abe

There are so many barriers that people face in connecting with biological ancestors, enslavement, genocide, and war among them. We've also talked about how whiteness as a construct takes away so many people's ancestors. In part, because of those barriers, it is important to remind ourselves that there are many ways to make and be family, and there are just as many ways to talk about ancestors and heritage.

I wanted to talk about cultural ancestors here in terms of "adopted ancestors" because I believe there are ancestors whose stories serve to encourage us even if we have no blood ties to them. So many people think DNA testing is the solution to a problem, and yet there are many reasons DNA testing doesn't accomplish what we hope it will.

- Results vary from company to company and vary over time, since companies are getting data by comparing it with other people in their data set, which changes based on who joins. (For example, a friend of mine got less accurate results from one of the top companies, which, because its earliest membership was heavily Mormon, had less data from people in Asia.)

- As one article put it, "DNA is not heritage." Because of how DNA is passed down (you don't get *all* of both parents' genes), you might have gotten more of your biological father's Slovak genes, while your sibling got more of his Turkish genes. Perhaps he got more of his father's Polish genes, while his sister got more of his Finnish genes. (Also, "European DNA" is kind of a misnomer anyway.)[51]

- Whoever has access to your DNA poses privacy risks depending on who has access to that data. One friend said she made the hard choice not to get her daughter a test because she didn't love the idea of DNA being able to be used against her daughter, given that junk science is already wielded against Black people so much as it is.

· · · · · · · · · · · · · · · · · · ·

> Creating a sense of "who we are" based on percentage of DNA from a place runs the risk of reinforcing the white supremacist practice of substituting science for culture and pretending that is enough.

I have friends who because of DNA tests connected with family they had never known or had been kept secret from each other, I have friends who have been able to re-connect with ancestral homelands or learned about their heritage prior to enslavement, which has given them new community and new relationships as a result. I have friends who learned about their biological parents because of it. Those have largely been gifts of connection previously not possible. But these tests do not, on the whole, answer the kinds of larger social questions we sometimes think they might.

DNA tests do not connect us to stories or culture or practices or ways of being of the people who came before us. In fact, creating a sense of "who we are" based on percentage of DNA from a place runs the risk of reinforcing the white supremacist practice of substituting science for culture and pretending that is enough. The most horrific example of

---

[51]https://www.vox.com/science-and-health/2019/1/28/18194560/ancestry-dna-23-me-myheritage-science-explainer

this is the white practice of determining Indigeneity through something called "blood quantum," or Blackness through the "one drop rule."

While I was working on this book, I immersed myself in the legendary epic *The Bruce Trilogy* by Neil Tranter. At the very beginning, there is a dramatic face-off between the Scottish clan chiefs and Edward I of England. It's enraging. It will make you resent England or royalty even more than you already do. I was good and mad, but then encountered this twist:

> Everywhere the cream of two nations bowed low, as Edward of England passed on . . . Or perhaps not quite the cream of two nations. For practically everyone in the church of Strathcaro that July day of 1296, save some of the humble men-at-arms, was of one stock—Norman-French . . . [Of all the lords and including the king, there was no English blood and almost no Scottish blood except Robert Bruce himself, who might at most have been half Scottish on his mother's side.] Every word in that church had been spoken in French. (Pp 23-24)

I was devastated.

I called my mother. I reminded her of this part of the book and asked if she had known that. She said she didn't remember it but wasn't shocked.

"I've always been confident because of how Scottish clans and Hindu castes work that I knew my heritage. Do you think I should get a DNA test?" I asked.

"Yeah," my mother responded, "you don't have to worry about that. It's not like our people came from lairds." In other words, don't forget who was born up a close.

Moreover, whatever my DNA reveals, what shapes me is a heritage passed down, a culture shaped by Celts and Picts, and possibly Vikings, all of whom lived together on the island of Great Cumbrae over 1,500 years ago. What shapes me is a culture itself shaped by hundreds of years of conflict with those to the South and more years of conflict with each other, a culture shaped by building community to survive bitter winters and get the most from what little was available to them. That's an ancestral culture that can serve me in this era of ecological and economic collapse when we will have to band together and do the most with what we have available. Those are ancestors, not biological but cultural, who offer me something I need for self-understanding and help create the future I need.

Even if some of those ancestors were French.

Cultural ancestors are a thing. I know this because of my tattoos. My first tattoo was a Celtic cross I got on my back when I got accepted into seminary at the age of twenty-six as a lifetime commitment to my cultural ancestors and my faith. When I was forty-five, my gift to myself was a multicolored tattoo on my upper thigh, a reproduction of an art piece by Indo-Trinidadian artist Shalini Seereeram. The tattoo was the image of two women wearing saris, entwined with each other in a horizontal embrace, as a commitment to my cultural ancestors and my queer identity. When I was about thirty-eight, I got a tattoo on my shoulder, which I call my "Oakland Peace Center tattoo" since it was a commitment to my cultural ancestors and to nonviolence and anti-imperialism. It's a spinning wheel (which played a distinct role in the fight for independence by what was then India and is now India/Pakistan/Bangladesh), with the word সত্যাগ্রহ or *Satyagraha*. Satyagraha is a term attributed to Mahatma Gandhi, loosely translated as "truth force," "soul force," or "love force," depending on how you understand Sanskrit. The term was created on South African soil by Gujaratis fighting the British in India.

The most famous of those Gujaratis was Mohandas K. Gandhi (referred to with the honorific Mahatma later in life), whose work for equal treatment began while he served as a lawyer in South Africa before returning to India to continue the work. Now that term marks a Bengali body. I can't imagine a DNA test would tie me to the Mahatma in any meaningful way, but this framework is no less a part of my legacy. The fact that people before me believed that the spiritual power of sacred truth could overcome a large and brutal empire (and proved it!) makes me feel less alone in the world.

I was raised with an implicit narrative that being Bengali was to study hard, do well in school, and be economically successful as a way of honoring those who came before you. I'm not sure this was ever said out loud; it's just that all of us kids who got raised going to Bengali parties in Akron on the weekends heard who got praised and who got whispered about, thousands of miles from Bengal. This was how we learned what it meant to be Bengali. It was only as I got closer to adulthood that I realized Bengalis had also been poets and freedom fighters and tragic romantics. (Bollywood movies always end happily; Bengali movies always end tragically.) And since learning the breadth of who Bengalis have been throughout history, I feel less out of place. I feel like I make a little more sense to myself. Beyond that, I feel a connection to a thread of resistance and questioning and justice-seeking that runs throughout Indian history despite the competing threads of oppressive power and pressure toward conformity for the sake of survival because while I studied hard and did well in school, my economic status is not "wealthy," and those drives to achievement seemed to limit more than motivate.

The TV show *Reservation Dogs*, which takes place on a Native American reservation in Oklahoma, offers another example of a cultural ancestor. The show's main character is a teenage boy feeling adrift after the death of his friend. What helps him set a path forward is a visitation by an ancestor who died at the battle of Little Bighorn. That character, William "Spirit" Knifeman, is maybe the funniest character in a show marked by dry wit throughout. He's a reminder that our cultural ancestors don't need to be glamorous or famous to offer us wisdom if we are willing to listen. They see things from a different vantage point that can help us make sense of our present.

In a gathering of a wisdom circle for people of color that shaped this book, one participant shared that they had found out they have Seminole heritage. They also knew, however, how that DNA ancestry so often gets fetishized by people in ways that don't actually honor the Indigenous people still in our midst and rarely lead to deep relationship with the Indigenous communities with whom they share DNA. "I long to delve into my Seminole heritage, but I'm wary," they said. "I don't want to cause harm. Who defines who is Native American? It's not usually Indigenous people."

Who defines our cultural ancestors? It's rarely the people whose cultural ancestors were suppressed, oppressed, rendered invisible, or erased.

The importance of our cultural ancestors isn't just who they are to us. Blood quantum, the determination of how Indigenous someone is based on the percentage of one nation's blood they carry, wasn't originally how most Indigenous nations understood belonging to community. Diverse native communities defined belonging in many ways, as they had numerous and distinct cultures, worldviews, and values. We'll talk more about that in later chapters, but it is worth noting that part of the value of cultural ancestors is learning different ways of understanding the world than we've been encouraged to by those around us. An author recently wrote a book telling the history of west Africa through oral traditions rather than relying on the much more predominant narratives by white Americans and Europeans. An article about the book's importance explained,

> Griots [essentially the storytellers, poets, and oral historians] of western Africa from Senegal and Mauritania across to Mali and Nigeria use oral traditions which date back over 2,000 years. They often accompany storytelling with musical instruments such as the Kora, a twenty-one stringed lute-bridge-harp, drums, or horns to tell stories. Similarly, elders from the region which is now modern-day Ghana, are steeped within the oral tradition and act as conduits of knowledge by passing down proverbs, some of which are reflected in Kente cloth print.
>
> As history presents· itself through the people, culture within West Africa shows itself to be dynamic and continuous. However, throughout history, the oral tradition has been dismissed by Western productions of knowledge. In essence, they have deprived the complexity of the oral tradition through presenting false written narratives about Africa which exclude lived experiences and draw on loaded colonial clichés.[52]

You've already heard one of the most important family stories to me, about my great grandmother who cried herself blind for love of her son. I had just heard that story on a trip to India in my mid-twenties when I returned to the US and shared it with a friend. He looked at me skeptically and said, "Ummm, yeah. She had glaucoma." Which is factually correct. But what I find more interesting in this case than a medical diagnosis is the reason we told that story. It told you something about us. That's what gets lost in foregrounding "western empiricism" as the primary lens through which to view the world. That's what gets taken from all of

---

[52]"West Africa's oral histories tell us a more complete story than traditional post-colonial narratives," Lavinya Stennet, December 16, 2019, Quartz Africa, https://qz.com/africa/1770108/west-africas-oral-history-griots-tell-a-more-complete-story

us relying solely on science: we lose the texture of our cultural ancestors, how they understood and created community.

If you haven't seen the documentary series "High on the Hog" on Netflix, you're missing out. The four episodes of season 1 cover so much of the heritage of African American cooking and how it has shaped our landscape.

In episode 3, "The Founding Chefs," the host, Stephen Satterfield, meets Gayle Jessup White, whose great-great-great-great uncle was James Hemings, the French-trained chef enslaved by Thomas Jefferson. Hemings was responsible for introducing macaroni and cheese to the United States.

Satterfield arrives on Jefferson's plantation in Virginia to try the original recipe of macaroni and cheese[53] and to ask White, who works on the staff of Monticello, to help us learn more about the Hemings family, and how it feels to be James Hemings's descendant. She responds, "It's really an honor. I'm lucky enough to know that history. But every Black American has something like that in their background. They just don't know it."

When Satterfield asks how she thinks her ancestors would feel about the overwhelming popularity of that beloved dish, White says:

> Gosh. Well, I'll tell you how I think about it. I'm kind of blown away by the idea that my ancestors helped originate this dish in the United States that has become an American staple. [tone change] I'm proud of the stamina they had, the determination they had, the character they had. I don't think anyone could imagine what it was like to live under those circumstances, knowing that you would never be free. They survived and then some. Because I'm standing here today. We're standing here today—and I get so emotional about this—because of them. Because of their strength. We're standing on their shoulders.
>
> This is nice. I like mac and cheese. We can use this as a symbol. But let's think of who those people really were, their strength, their character, their endurance. So yeah, I'm super proud. Not just because I'm descended from them but because they represent the very best of the United States of America.[54]

---

[53] (spoiler: they boil the pasta in milk and it is a game changer)
[54] *High on the Hog*, season 1 episode 3, approximately minute 33.

You may already have gleaned that this book isn't really written for people who think they're doing fine and don't need their ancestors. Here, though, I will be explicit: with a world as hard to navigate, as violent and oppressive, and as isolating as this one, I actually think it's pretty arrogant to think we don't need ancestors in order to get through this life and attempt to make the world better for those who come after us. I think it is foolish to write off the wisdom of people who came before. I even think it's a product of white supremacy culture, which cuts us off from those who came before and shames us for not being able to do on our own something that none of us could do on our own and still emerge with our souls intact.

Despite my convictions about the wisdom of ancestors, so much of our culture denigrates so many of our ancestors. Doing the work of recognizing our cultural ancestors' wisdom may be a way of fighting back against white supremacy, whether we are white people or people of color.

My friend Ashe told me a story of a time during her childhood when her mother got sick. Word got around that small town, and in no time, they had hundreds of pounds of food at their door. "There was a baked-in assumption of hospitality," Ashe said. "Everything wasn't amazing after that. The moral codes still showed up in our community, the judgments and whispers, but there was a sense of community, people connecting at the corner store. The downtowns are boarded up now in a lot of rural America, and with those disappearing downtowns is a loss of what roots people had. Poor rural white people have wisdom for middle-class white people. But we have to recognize the remnants of wisdom we have."

I mentioned in a previous chapter the horrific things that famed anti-fascist folk singer Woody Guthrie's father did in Oklahoma. My friend, who described himself as "a mutt" and is from Oklahoma, might not be shocked to learn about that awful piece of history. He knows a lot about the harm that white Oklahomans did to both the Black community and the Indigenous community on that land. But what does it mean that Woody Guthrie is part of his cultural legacy as much as Charley Guthrie is? What does it mean for white people who don't know their biological ancestry to recognize cultural ancestors who resisted? Who could we be if we learned more about people from our communities who saw evil and stood against it in small and big ways, people like Woody Guthrie but also people who refused to join the Confederacy or the "No-No Boys" in the Japanese incarceration camps in the US during World War II who resisted the hypocrisy of the US government quietly but staunchly? What if we took strength from those stories as well as the stories of how they struggled and how they survived, and how they took care of each other and settled disputes and honored their dead? What if we also sought out the stories of cultural ancestors who built cross-racial solidarity? If we ask the right questions, we sometimes discover answers that wouldn't have surfaced otherwise.

In 2019, Art Spiegelman wrote an article about how superhero comic books were launched by people committed to anti-fascism. You may know Spiegelman's name (as I do) because his groundbreaking long-form comic books *Maus* and *Maus II* transformed how comic books are understood as a literary art form. Spiegelman himself does not love the term graphic novel because he doesn't think we should have looked down on comic books in the first place. And here's why: the creators of Superman were young Jewish New Yorkers who created a hero who would stand up against Nazis, fascists, and racists, a hero whose very commitment to fighting those forms of evil were what made him American. In the article, Spiegelman goes on to say:

> At this point, it might be worth pointing out (not out of ethnic pride, but because it might shed some light on the rawness and the specific themes of the early comics) that the pioneers behind this embryonic medium based in New York were predominantly Jewish and from ethnic minority backgrounds. It wasn't just Siegel and Shuster, but a whole generation of recent immigrants and their children, those most vulnerable to the ravages of the great depression, who were especially attuned to the rise of virulent antisemitism in Germany. They created the American Übermenschen[55] who fought for a nation that would at least nominally welcome "your tired, your poor, your huddled masses yearning to breathe free . . ."[56]

---

[55]"Übermensch" was a term originally coined by Friedrich Nietzsche to describe the ideal man who could impose a culture on a people by strength of will and character.

[56]"Art Spiegelman: golden age superheroes were shaped by the rise of fascism," Art Spiegelman, The Guardian, August 17, 2019. https://www.theguardian.com/books/2019/aug/17/art-spiegelman-golden-age-superheroes-were-shaped-by-the-rise-of-fascism?fbclid=IwAR2PPHED_Op_eTKqn0vWZoNVQC619EPMuI-f5AqUnxEDJ6rLQygHDiCdPrLg

A lot of these artists had to change their names to get hired or published in the rampant antisemitism of the US, but their heroes fought for a day they wouldn't have to.

Here is where I want to do what the fancy people would call a bit of "hermeneutics."[57] Spiegelman's story about those early comic book artists is factually correct. If he had written the article in 2012, I would have been interested. In fact, I learned about the Jewish creators of Superman in the late 1990s and did find it a cool piece of history. But the reason he writes about it in 2019 is because this country was in the grips of the most visible bout of antisemitic, anti-immigrant, anti-Muslim, anti-Black, anti-queer, anti-Indigenous, anti-poor, anti-woman federal leadership in the last thirty or fifty or one hundred and fifty years, give or take. By writing that article a year after a mass shooting of a synagogue in Pittsburgh, in a year of increased anti-Jewish vandalism and hate crimes in Europe as well as the US, Spiegelman was offering a way forward by evoking important cultural ancestors for a distinct moment. He was offering a word of encouragement to young people from his own Jewish American community, that their ancestors had redefined American power for a generation.

> The way our cultural ancestors show up for us and how and why we need them changes greatly based on what we're facing individually and collectively.

One of my favorite ancestors was a futurist. A few years back, my friends Anirvan and Barnali coordinated a progressive South Asian cultural showcase at the San Francisco Asian American Museum. One of the performances introduced me to a feminist sci-fi short story from 1905. The author was a Bengali woman raised in a traditional family that expected her to live in Zenana[58] with the women living separate from the men and only allowed to learn Arabic in order to read the Qur'an. Rokeya Sakhawat Hossain's story "Sultana's Dream" imagined a world

---

[57]Hermeneutics is a term that basically means "looking at the social location of the person who's analyzing something further back in history." So, the way someone in the 1970s talked about dinosaurs looks different than the way someone in the 21st century talks about them, not just because we have more science but because our worldview has changed.

[58]Zenana are the inner apartments in a home that were specifically for the women, in times when women were kept separate from men in royal families in India, particularly during the Mughal dynasty.

where men instead were cloistered off so women could research for health and wellness instead of greed and conquest.[59]

While my family is Hindu, I'm aware of the cultural realities of sexism that aren't just about religion. Something about this story reverberated in my soul and made me connect with ancestors in a different way, having watched some of my female family members not getting to live the lives they were gifted to live. Connecting with that cultural ancestor opened my heart and my imagination and also my awareness of what my ancestors could see that I didn't realize they could see.

On the one hand, I roll my eyes when someone says, "We're all from the same race, the human race." On the other hand, my colleague BK is pushing a very different boundary when he says to a mixed-race group, "Everyone in here is African American." What he's saying is we all come from Africa if we trace our lineage back far enough, which means the anti-Blackness of this country is irrational and ultimately self-loathing. I do not think he would be excited about non-Black people appropriating Black culture, but he wouldn't complain if we started to treat Black people as family. (The cousin we love, not the uncle we try to sit as far as possible from at family reunions.)

Here is some *fascinating* data that gives me pause about whose culture I claim. In 2016, *Royal Society Open Science* published an article about archaeologists' research into some beloved fairytales dating back 2,500-6,000 years ago.[60] Because of how languages branch out from one another, it's possible to trace stories by saying, "Oh, this fairytale showed up in these two very different locations . . . they share the same language of origin back this many years ago." As a result, *Beauty and the Beast*, for example, shows up in variations all over the world because of three things, the scientists argue: (a) a common language going back millennia, (b) enough magic to make it memorable (transformation), and (c) values significant enough to stand the test of time (don't judge people by their looks, prioritize family needs, etc.).

---

[59]"Feminist Visions of Science and Utopia in Rokeya Sakhawat Hossain's 'Sultana's Dream,'" Lady Science, 2019, https://www.ladyscience.com/features/feminist-visions-science-fiction-utopia-rokeya-hossain?fbclid=IwAR2jLn7bGpV27 74IPfUPH8goXdRbG2tFo-KQ4blVhiKBFOGm_dNMaTiLrCM

[60]"Some fairy tales may be 6,000 years old." David Schultz, Science, April 22, 2016. https://www.science.org/content/article/some-fairy-tales-may-be-6000-years-old

We have diverse and multiple cultures, though, don't we?

In previous chapters, we talked about how ableism had created so much for us to grieve. Anti-ableist ancestors can give encouragement to people with disabilities, but they also offer gifts to non-disabled people that are also critical since ableism distorts all our relationships with each other.

In a beautiful essay on how learning about disabled ancestors helped her form a different relationship to her own daughter's autism diagnosis, Jennifer Natalya Fink writes:

> Our disability lineages can only be reclaimed through the stories we uncover. This means conceiving of disability as an identity like being queer, rather than reducing it to a medical condition. L.G.B.G.T.Q.+ people such as myself, who in the closeted past had no queer family members to look to as models, can now proudly find and claim their queer lineage, reclaiming and retelling family narratives to include their queer ancestors. Despite this progress, disability remains stigmatized. Disabled forbears often remain in the shadows, viewed with shame, not pride. Without ancestry, family history, or lineage. Inconceivable.[61]

She goes on to talk about how we might uncover those ancestors hidden from us, and while she is talking about biological ancestors, what she shares feels germane to all the ancestors whose stories are hidden, biological or otherwise:

> Finding disability lineage can mean learning to listen. To hear the untold story in euphemisms, silences, and gaps. To read between the family lines. . . . Reclaiming our disability lineage also means rethinking fundamentally what a disability is, its meaning and value. I had never thought of my Grandma Adina as disabled. I just knew she adored me, dance in any form, and social justice, possibly in that order. Grandma Adina was also extremely hard of hearing. Yet I never thought of her as part of my family's rich disability lineage. Nor did I let, as Jewish tradition enjoins, her disabled memory be a blessing for my daughter. Shame and stigma about disability are so great that

---

[61]https://www.nytimes.com/2022/02/27/opinion/disabled-ancestry-family-pride.html

I had internalized them, never acknowledging that my dynamic dancing grandma was disabled.[62]

I mentioned in the last chapter the grief I carry for Keshn Singh and Jamil Singh and Rola Singh, three of the Indian farm workers arrested in the US for having sex with other men in the early 1900s, and how that grief deepened my self-understanding as a queer person and South Asian immigrant almost a century later.

But in doing the same research, while I am certain there must be lost stories of queer South Asian women from this same time, I haven't surfaced them yet. So as I try to sort out the acceptable parameters of who is an ancestor (and I'm still figuring out what those parameters are for me), if I can broaden my queer female and genderqueer immigrant ancestors as wide as I want, I want to claim Dr. Mae Chung, the first American surgeon of Chinese descent, who dressed in truly dapper style and drove a sleek blue sports car around San Francisco in the 1920s and who was rumored to have had an affair with legendary actress, comedienne and singer Sophie Tucker, one of the most popular US entertainers in the first half of the 20th century, while they raised funds for the boys fighting in World War II. I think part of why she calls out to me is she radiates little longing, no apology, and lots of joy.

I also want to claim as an ancestor another gay man whose life looked a lot different than those of Keshn and Jamil and Rola Singh, because he is a much more recent ancestor. Iftakhar Naseem founded Sangat, a South Asian LGBTQ+ organization in Chicago in the 1980s. He brought together culture and community and ancestors and queerness lived out loud. In a tribute to him on NBC Asian America to honor him after his death, the following quote from the beloved "Ifti" seemed to capture his commitment to the same work I do today. "At first, when you come to America you deny your heritage. And I denied my heritage for a long time. But then I realized if you don't know where you come from, you don't know where you're going."[63]

[62]https://www.nytimes.com/2022/02/27/opinion/disabled-ancestry-family-pride.html

[63]https://www.saada.org/tides/article/paving-the-way-for-cyber-queens

Indigenous people so often do not get to self-define. I'm grateful for this wisdom from Laurie Jones Neighbors, again reflecting on the book *Prosperity and American Conquest: Indian Women of the Ohio River Valley, 1690-1792* by Susan Sleeper-Smith.

> Thanks to so-called "Westward Expansion," the Shawnee tribe is splintered, and Shawnee people are small in numbers, but Shawnees are working hard to revitalize language and cultural traditions that were difficult to hold on to after "removal" from the Ohio River Valley. Yet, one of my Blue Jacket cousins once told me that when she is asked how she feels about being so assimilated (an observation, I think, that must be in response to Blue Jacket out-marriage, first with French traders and later, after forced location to Kansas, with European immigrants and American settlers in Indian Territory), she points to the experiences of those who did not assimilate and says she is glad that our family was able to survive.
>
> Sleeper-Smith might take issue with that—the idea that our family has merely assimilated—and I am able to see her point after re-envisioning Shawnee and other Algonquian-speaking women in the Ohio River Valley. We are so much more than assimilated. We are additive, cumulative, evolving. Even when it appears that we are assimilating, we are not stepping out of our skin and becoming something else—we are constantly becoming something more, while always bringing our ancestors forward with us.[64]

You can probably tell by now how much love I have for other people's cultural ancestors. I think that learning about others' ancestors gives me a different clarity about my own. "Ohhhh, those cultural ancestors cultivated humor as a way of managing pain; I think my cultural ancestors used a little more spiritual practice of acceptance of one's fate. I love that humor helped them so much," is an example of my self-revelation as I encounter others' cultural ancestors and reflect on them relative to my own.

---

[64]https://citiesandpeople.com/ljnc-blog/2019/6/19/1100-silver-brooches-and-a-tool-for-thinking-about-transformative-change

There are also times I find myself connecting with or resonating with an ancestral story because I have lived on the land where it unfolded. People know that I rep Akron, Ohio hard. I wasn't born there. My people aren't from there. My people don't live there now and probably aren't going to live there again. But the working people (and the wanted-to-be-working people in that rust belt town in the post-industrial US) of Akron reminded me of my mother's post-industrial town of Airdrie, on the edges of Glasgow. And you'll hear me talk about "our proud heritage" in Akron *a lot*. My commitment to labor justice came from the ancestors in that town as well as the people I grew up with.

This gets messy. Lots of non-Native people, for example, believe they have a unique relationship to Indigenous people because of a vibe, and it results in practicing rituals that aren't theirs. People claim affinities to ancestral practices and traditions in ways that are out of relationship with the communities whose practices they adopt. This ends up being a way of exploiting people and not building up solidarity. Usually this results when people want the trappings of someone else's cultural ancestors without forming relationship to those communities in any meaningful way.

On the other hand, sometimes the claiming of others' cultural ancestors can be part of how relationship is formed. I led a prayer session for an online community called The Chapel in the summer of 2021, and one of the attendees messaged me afterward. It turned out she was also from Airdrie, the town where my mother grew up (when she wasn't spending every break and summer with her gran in Millport). She talked about a trip she had made to an ancient Scottish battleground. She heard someone telling his family about why this battlefield was "such a critical part of our history." When she turned around, she saw that he was South Asian and Sikh. She was *delighted*, and proud that he saw this battleground and this country as his. So proud that she wanted to make sure I heard about it years later.

A number of years ago I got to visit Australia. My favorite part of that amazing trip was a little weekend trip in the Blue Mountains, maybe a two-hour train ride from Sydney. I spent a day on an "Aboriginal walkabout," where an Aboriginal man led us through the forest to a waterfall, telling us about what a spirit quest would have been like for an Aboriginal person as their coming-of-age process. (He was very clear that we were not engaging in a spirit quest ourselves since we weren't part of that community, and he was doing this to educate rather than to let people play out some inappropriate fantasy.)[65]

· · · · · · · · · · · · · · · · · · · ·

We can honor and receive the gifts of each other's cultural ancestors as a way of fueling our own work, recognizing that they don't belong to us and yet they inform us.

At the very beginning of our day together, he shared that while he was from an Aboriginal community on the other side of the continent, Aboriginal people believe that you belong to the community on whose land you live, so he was active in and was considered a part of the Aboriginal community there in the Blue Mountains.

I wonder what it would mean for us to understand ourselves as belonging to, being accountable to, being in relationship with the ancestors of the land on which we find ourselves. More of that in a future chapter, but for now, I offer that as a possible construct for how we can engage cultural ancestors who are not ours: engaging them in ways that are relational and accountable if we want to belong to those ancestors in a serious way. In the midst of that, we can honor and receive the gifts of each other's cultural ancestors as a way of fueling our own work, recognizing that they don't belong to us and yet they inform us.

I once got to hear a beautiful performance by a Polish musician. She said her life as a touring musician could be lonely but was never boring. She spent her time practicing and reading. She said one of the books she had been loving recently was *Les Misérables*, because it reminded her that across history and culture, we are united in our desire for peace and liberty. She was raised during Poland's struggle for liberty. She said she had parents who raised her to fight for and to value freedom. One of her heroes was electrician and Nobel peace prize winner Lech Walesa, whose work for the Polish Solidarity movement helped bring down communism in the late 1980s and who embodied the same values Victor Hugo had written about so many years before.

---

[65]The best part of this walkabout was when he told us to roll eucalyptus leaves into little balls to put in our nostrils as the people of the community did for its healing properties. It smelled awesome, but to this day I'm not 100% sure he wasn't having us on.

She played "I Dreamed a Dream" from the musical *Les Mis*. Then, in tribute to other ancestors who also embodied the desire for peace and liberty, she played "Hava Negila."

May we learn about our cultural ancestors. Whether we know biological ancestors or not, our cultural ancestors can expand our future possibilities. And may we learn about and be nourished by one another's ancestors appreciatively and accountably, and not with appropriation, that they may help us understand our own ancestors better and deepen our relationships across diversity and difference, that we may feel ever more connected.

Where We Can Go from Here

○ *If you want to write and reflect on this chapter's theme in your own life:*

Gayle Jessup talked about how macaroni and cheese might be a metaphor for her ancestors, their strength, character, endurance. As you look at some of the ancestors you treasure from your cultural background, reflect on the object that might be a metaphor for the gifts they have to offer.

○ *If you want to engage a personal ritual around this chapter's theme:*

Print out and tape up images of ancestors from your cultural background. Write on the printout a word that you associate with them. Every day for a week, take a moment to pause and thank them. Let them know how you're carrying on their work.

○ *If you want to engage your activist or spiritual group in a practice that will help them begin to connect with ancestors in new ways as part of their work to dismantle white supremacy:*

Share with each other the cultural ancestors that mean the most to you and why. Each of you take someone else's favorite cultural ancestor home and give thanks for them every day for a week.

Chapter Seven

Movement Ancestors

We must wake up to the insane reality of our time. We are all irresponsible, unless we demand from the responsible decision makers that modern armaments must no longer be made available to people whose former battle axes and swords our ancestors condemned.

—*Thor Heyerdahl*

At this point in my life, I see how the Highland Clearances and the breaking apart of kinship commitments shape my work today around anti-displacement. The experiences of those biological and cultural ancestors shape me.

At this point in my life, I know that the Cellular Jail in the Andaman Islands that I visited with my parents stands as a testament to the thousands of brave Bengali resisters who stood against violent British colonialism and lost their freedom, families, and homelands as a result. Those cultural ancestors give me courage when I'm asked to risk incarceration in solidarity with fast food workers standing up against the people exploiting them.

A long time ago, I didn't know those stories. I saw the movie *Gandhi* in first grade (my friends said I was lying that the movie was three hours long; their collected data suggested that movies were ninety minutes and animated). Four years later, in fifth grade, we learned about Martin Luther King, Jr.

Our history book said Dr. King was influenced by Gandhi, who had been influenced by Thoreau. In a Black and White world in Akron, Ohio in the 1980s, white wasn't quite the right fit for little bi-racial, South Asian Sandhya. Dr. King seemed to have liked my people, so I decided Dr. King was my people, too, and his movement was my movement. I read every book in the school library about him. One book had the sheet music to "We Shall Overcome," which I made my music teacher play for me after class one day so I would know what it sounded like. Although I couldn't really know what it sounded like until I heard people sing it and mean it, their ancestors' struggle coming out in the notes and the pauses and the hums.

In eighth grade, we learned about Cesar Chavez.

In eleventh grade, the movie *Malcolm X* came out.

I now live in a community that helps me understand that King and Chavez and Malcolm X are not mine to claim. At the same time, those ancestors also help me understand what's possible and what people facing different challenges can do and did do. They help me ponder what my role in my own community is, learning from their lessons how my work can serve our contemporary movements and also learning how my community might show up better for theirs. They also remind me to be aware of my own limits because they all had flaws and imperfections and faults.

Our ancestors may be a complex gift we have to honor well, but they are a gift.

⊰⊰⊰⊰⊰⊰   ⊱⊱⊱⊱⊱⊱

As we talked about in the first section of the book, we sometimes get very limited glimpses into who our biological ancestors were. The ones who stood out might get erased. The ones deemed successful by this warped society's views get venerated. The ones who suffered in silence get lifted up as models. The ones who resisted become cautionary tales or get ignored.

For that reason, movement ancestors can provide a glimpse into where we come from that our family trees might try to hide. I'll be honest: the categories of cultural ancestors, movement ancestors and spiritual ancestors can get a bit blurry, so I'll note that in this chapter. I'm going to try to wrestle with what it means to engage ancestors who aren't probably our biological ancestors and may or may not be our cultural ancestors but who show us what it looks like to resist oppression. Here, we will look to these ancestors for their help in ways that give us a model, give us a community, or simply give us a boost when we're feeling defeated.

This is why movement ancestors matter so much to me. I encounter people all the time who feel defeated. Some of them have given years to the movement for justice. Some of them don't do anything at all for the movement for justice because they grew up in the shadow of Watergate or Iran-Contra, Clarence Thomas, or *Too Big to Fail*, the Gulf Wars or the war in Afghanistan, and Citizens United or diminishing voting access for people of color. For those doing the work in any number of communities over the last forty years, their lived experience shows them pretty clearly that things almost always, inevitably, get worse.

One of my living movement heroes is the Rev. Dr. William Barber of the current day Poor People's Campaign. He often talks about how we are in the third reconstruction. The first was after the Civil War. The second was the US Freedom Movement (sometimes called the Civil Rights movement). And here we are today, living in and creating the third.

When Dr. Barber talks about those two previous reconstructions, he evokes ancestors, and he evokes eras. Many of us know enough about history to have a glimpse into how horrific things were for Black people and how powerful those two movements were. People in this country have suffered horrors. They have faced governments completely and universally committed to denying their full rights and full humanity, and they have won.

> People in this country have suffered horrors. They have faced governments completely and universally committed to denying their full rights and full humanity, and they have won.

Connecting with those movement ancestors, listening for what wisdom they have to offer the movement in which you find yourself, is pure gift. Listening to them tell you that it *is* worth standing for something even when you think nothing will change could completely re-orient what you do with your life.

I mentioned in a previous chapter that my friend Cisa invited our group of people of color activists to think about which ancestor we wanted to confront with the harm they had caused. She also asked us which ancestor we wanted to thank and for what. Inspired, I asked that question in one of the white peoples' wisdom circles, and one participant said, without hesitation, "The Grimke sisters and Anne Braden."[66] Both, in different ways and at different times, had stood as best they could in their contexts for an end to white supremacy culture and for the alternative of justice. For that participant, those ancestors showed that white women could play an important and (particularly in the case of Anne Braden) self-reflective role in the work of racial justice.

I don't have much of a stomach for romcoms. Those aren't the movies that pull at my heartstrings. But when I watched the movie *Pride*, which tells of the ways Welsh miners showed up to fight for LGBTQ rights after LGBTQ activists had fought for the miners, I pretended I had a cold, but everyone knew what that sniffling was about. In the 2015 movie *Trumbo*, when blacklisted screenwriter Dalton Trumbo is presented by his peers with a lifetime achievement award after being shut out of the movie industry for his commitment to economic justice during the Red Scare, I didn't even pretend I had a cold that time. I just wept.

There's something about knowing what other people went through, and how they made it through, and how they showed up for each other and fought for each other, that makes me feel less alone and less daunted. So, yeah, I indulge occasionally in imagining Dalton Trumbo cheering me on as I write and work.

I already quoted the essay by Stacey Park/Milbern on disability justice and what she called "crip ancestors." This part of her essay feels essential to this chapter and why movement ancestors matter to our current day work of justice.

> I think about crip ancestorship often. It is tied to crip eldership for me, a related but different topic. So many disabled people live short lives, largely because of social determinants of health

---

[66]Angelina and Sarah Grimke were among the first white women to publicly speak out in favor of abolition in the early 1800s, supporting full racial and gender equality. Anne Braden was a white civil rights activist and journalist throughout the second half of the twentieth century.

like lack of healthcare, housing, clean air and water, or having basic needs met. Other times the short lives are merely one truth of our bodyminds, like the neuromuscular conditions Harriet, Laura, and I have. I do not know a lot about spirituality or what happens when we die, but my crip queer Korean life makes me believe that our earthly bodyminds is but a fraction, and not considering our ancestors is electing only to see a glimpse of who we are. People sometimes assume ancestorship is reserved for those of biological relation, but a queered or cripped understanding of ancestorship holds that, such as in flesh, our deepest relationships are with people we choose to be connected to and honor day after day.[67]

I think frequently about what those miners and LGBTQ+ activists in Britain would want you to know about how to do your work of solidarity. I literally pause and listen when I do this. I have this very real sense they want us to get better at showing up for each other. They understand why we distrust each other; so did they. It might be because I've hung out with my share of working-class Brits and I'm projecting, but I get a sense that they're not very patient with our wordsmithing and expectation that everyone will understand us perfectly and get things right all the time in order for us to work with them. I get a sense from them that they think this work is too urgent for us to feel tepid or beleaguered or nihilistic about it.

And I'm not 100 percent sure I'm really channeling anyone so much as I know a bit of history and a bit of culture, and I have a sense of the energy of the people who lived through those seemingly hopeless miners' campaigns and who were out activists during the height of the AIDS crisis. But whatever it is that's happening, I know I engage my work differently when I stop and listen to them.

I'm not the only person I know who has learned from other movement (and biological) ancestors about showing up in solidarity. When I started grad school for my ministerial degree, I was in a class with John, a white guy who sported an Amish beard. We were in our twenties, and the dude was *not* Amish but there he was. I did not know what to make of him. As I got to know him, though, I realized he

---

[67]https://disabilityvisibilityproject.com/2019/03/10/on-the-ancestral-plane-crip-hand-me-downs-and-the-legacy-of-our-movements/

had tons of integrity. He didn't say much, though what he did say was almost always either bitingly funny or staggeringly insightful. Instead, John lived his beliefs. He had come to grad school after serving at a social service program in the small city of Evansville, Indiana that was multiracial, multi-class, and incredibly challenging as well as beautiful. While we went to a school that definitely prioritized an academic track, one thing we had in common was we both ultimately sought out less glamorous ministries that would let us be who we were, me in northern California building on what I had learned in a ministry internship with post-incarcerated gang members in Los Angeles, and John returning to Patchwork Central in Evansville (and getting a nursing degree, as if he was just trying to make the rest of us look like slackers).

The thing that made John so cool in hindsight was that he wasn't interested in being cool; he was interested in being connected. For him, that meant staying connected to who he came from.

I always thought that connection manifested most obviously in his Ozark-inspired harmonica and bluegrass fiddle playing and, you know, the beard. But John notes that it was his mother's leadership in the Blind Civil Rights Movement—as someone with a child as well as family of choice who were blind—that shaped his family even more. I have to say, he taught all of us in that class to deepen our disability analysis. That said, he shared this in response to my assessment.

> I do think that my mom growing up extremely poor in rural Ozark country was key to *her* sense of justice and solidarity, because she very much knew what it was like to go through hard times and she had that keen-yet-tough empathy that drove her to show up for others who were having hard times, especially other parents of blind children.

There are few people I trust more to show up well in the work of racial justice than John. Believe me, I know that correlation is not causation. I don't think John's connection to his heritage or other justice movements automatically positioned him for solidarity with the fight against mass incarceration. But it did mean that when he showed up, he showed up with a lot less racial anxiety, and he showed up with a sense of what it means to have gone through hard things and to make sure when others are going through hard things, you . . . well, you show up.

Maybe the second conversation I had about this book was with a friend, a white person, who thought my topic was great for people of color but maybe not great for white people, whose ancestors had created the mess with which we currently live. "But I think that's the problem," I said. "This construct of whiteness means that even in the midst of anti-racism work, y'all aren't allowed to connect with your movement ancestors." When she asked whom I meant, I named the indentured servants in Bacon's Rebellion, the striking coal miners in West Virginia, and before I could continue, she said, "But those are all poor and working-class examples."

Right.

And that's maybe the reason movement ancestors matter so much to me. The statistical odds are that most of us come from poor and working-class ancestors. Even if we don't, and even if we don't know if we did, we can still connect with and learn from the ancestors who resisted, the ancestors who created something better, the ancestors who build bridges instead of walls, the ancestors who created community.

There's a quote I both love and hate because it's so true, often misattributed to John Steinbeck because he was someone who understood class in a country that actively seeks to deny its existence (and because he said things very similar to this). The quote goes, "Socialism never took root in America because the poor see themselves not as an exploited proletariat but as temporarily embarrassed millionaires."[68]

---

[68]The delightful tumblr account "Hell Yes, John Steinbeck" explains the misattribution of the quote this way:

As quoted in A Short History of Progress (2005) by Ronald Wright, p. 124; though this has since been cited as a direct quote by some, the remark may simply be a paraphrase, as no quotation marks appear around the statement and earlier publication of this phrasing have not been located.

This is likely an incorrect quote from America & Americans, 1966:

"Except for the field organizers of strikes, who were pretty tough monkeys and devoted, most of the so-called Communists I met were middle-class, middle-aged people playing a game of dreams. I remember a woman in easy circumstances saying to another even more affluent: 'After the revolution even we will have more, won't we, dear?' Then there was another lover of proletarians who used to raise hell with Sunday picknickers on her property.

"I guess the trouble was that we didn't have any self-admitted proletarians. Everyone was a temporarily embarrassed capitalist. Maybe the Communists so closely questioned by the investigation committees were a danger to America, but the ones I knew—at least they claimed to be Communists—couldn't have disrupted a Sunday-school picnic. Besides they were too busy fighting among themselves."

https://hellyesjohnsteinbeck.tumblr.com/post/23486952183/commonly-misquoted-socialism-never-took-root-in

Steinbeck's observation matters because as James Baldwin, another prophetic literary voice, says, "What passes for identity in this country is a series of myths about one's heroic ancestors."[69] We embrace the narratives of overromanticized ancestors, narratives that do not ultimately empower us or bring us together in healthy ways.

It's not embarrassed millionaires or heroic ancestors who shaped the past. The past is shaped by collections of people, and those collections of people build on each other in ways we don't always see because we have been trained to have a very narrow definition of success.

Sometimes in anti-racism workshops I lead, I include an exercise where people actively engage the history of race in the United States. Something I've learned is that this timeline inspires and motivates me, whereas it often overwhelms and depresses others. Partly that's because I learned those pieces of history over the course of decades and created the timeline based on which parts of our nation's history speak to me. So I see how Plessy v. Ferguson in the 1880s made room for Ozawa v. US in 1922, which made room for Thind v. US in 1923, slowly building a case for how ridiculous racial paradigms for citizenship were, leading to things like the 1964 Civil Rights Act and 1965 Immigration Rights Act and my own path to citizenship.

All of those cases demonstrated the slow and steady pressure on the Supreme Court to resolve the horrors it had exacerbated in the Dred Scott case in 1858. The reason I got motivated to learn those stories is that in an anti-racism training I attended over twenty years ago, Thind v. US showed up on their timeline. In learning about that case, I discovered that people like me not only lived on this land long before my parents' friends in Akron (all of us were first-generation immigrants in the 1980s), but there had been people like me who fought for justice, demanding that this country figure out what it actually meant by citizens, what it actually meant by race, and what it actually owed its people, whoever those people were.

I first got engaged in the labor movement in the 1990s. My mother and I read a book called *Which Side Are You On* by Thomas Geoghegan. The book covered Geohegan's efforts to fight for labor rights in the United States in the 1970s and 1980s, when organized labor looked

---

[69]https://www.zinnedproject.org/materials/baldwin-talk-to-teachers I know I keep saying this, but you should read this whole talk. It is brilliant and powerful and absolutely peak Baldwin.

like it might never win again, following intense anti-union legislation at the federal and state levels. (This is why the subtitle of his book was "Being for Labor When It's Flat on Its Back.") Now, while reviewers at the time found it a quirky and charming memoir of a labor loyalist, my mother read it and for years after pointed to it as an example of how we were never going to win the fight for workers' rights. It robbed her of all hope.

Reading of these hard years, my mother had a distinct sense of "Why did we bother when it all led here?" She despaired as she looked at the Clinton administration, which actively devalued labor in order to prop up global trade that some leaders thought would strengthen the US, but ultimately only strengthened people who were already wealthy. Given that view, it's hard to blame her.

But today, across Appalachia, teachers and miners and environmental activists are demanding work with dignity and preservation of the land. Their fight is guided by the history of the Harlan County miners' strike in the 1930s, the strikes to preserve hospitals in 1965, and the teachers' strike of 1971. In fact, one modern-day protester stated, "Often the story is told as the federal government swoops in and is telling people what to do, but in fact, this came from protests around Washington, D.C., and in the region because of the hospital closures."[70]

Correcting the story to include those connections matters; those connections to movement ancestors are critical to our own work. I used to teach a course on social justice and theology. I broke the class into three groups to research three different movements from the 1990s. One was the resistance to welfare reform in DC, one was the WTO protests in Seattle, and one was the Zapatista rebellion in Chiapas. I asked them to find ways the religious community was involved (often they couldn't, even though I knew religious leaders in all three movements . . . and Catholic priests' involvement is literally part of the Wikipedia entry about the Zapatistas). I asked them to connect those campaigns to the growth of neoliberalism, which we were studying. I asked them to name how those campaigns had influenced later movements (again they couldn't, even though some of them were involved in the Poor People's Campaign or the Fight for Fifteen or had even been part of Occupy Wall Street).

---

[70]"Appalachia's Deep History of Resistance," Mason Adams, *Yes* magazine, September 26, 2019.

I sound unduly harsh about my students when this was in no way their fault; in fact, experiencing the difficulty of tracing throughlines was part of the point of the exercise. We are not trained to see connections in history, so of course we can't connect with movement ancestors. We're discouraged from knowing that they're there. We're discouraged from knowing they have things to offer. We're discouraged from noticing that they were part of emerging movements, and so it is hard for us to see where we might also be part of emerging movements.

Rabbi Danya Rutenberg, another contemporary movement leader, regularly delves into history, especially history in the Jewish Bible, in order to teach, to reveal and make plain, the connections between overlooked spiritual ancestors (next chapter) and overlooked movement ancestors. She reminds us that those ancestors encourage, support, and move us best when we actually know about them.

In this essay, she connects the exodus from Egypt and the songs of Moses and Miriam and the movement dynamics in the wilderness with the movement US freedom several millennia later.

> It seems that the Song—perhaps first existing as part of an oral tradition—may originally have been ascribed to Miriam, who led the Israelites in a powerful call-and-response of praise and worship—and that she may have later been cut and pasted out of the top of the Song to give Moses a more prominent role.

> Movements do this. It's entirely possible, probable, even, that Miriam was there, there at the start, even if she was ultimately pasted to the end of the Song as a post-script. Because it suited another agenda to center Moses.

> I'm drawn to think about Claudette Colvin and Rosa Parks here, for some reason.

> Most people know of Rosa Parks, the woman whose arrest in December 1955 for refusing to cede her seat to a white passenger famously kicked off the Montgomery Bus Boycott. But she wasn't the first.

> In March of that same year, nine months before Parks' arrest, a fifteen-year-old Black teenager named Claudette Colvin did the same thing. She was on a bus with some friends that day, and the driver asked several of them to get up so that a white

woman could sit. But, as Colvin recounts, "History had me glued to the seat. Harriet Tubman's hands were pushing down on one shoulder and Sojourner Truth's hands were pushing down on the other shoulder."

She was dragged off the bus and thrown into an adult jail. Several other Black people arrested before Colvin had also been arrested for refusing to give up their seats, but she was the first to ask to retain a lawyer, to try to fight back.

The local chapter of the NAACP arranged representation for her and initially thought hers could be a great case to challenge bus segregation, but the leadership team changed their plan upon learning that she was pregnant.

There were two extremely practical concerns—that conservative churches wouldn't rally behind an "unwed mother," and that without the churches, there would be no boycott; and that the white media would have a field day with the optics and use it to discount the movement entirely. (This might be the case, still, today. And remember, this was the Jim Crow South in 1955.)

Rosa Parks first met Colvin about two weeks after the teenager's arrest, and was in touch with her regularly, as Parks was then the secretary of the local NAACP branch. Colvin's arrest indeed inspired her own actions. ...

Notably, Colvin was one of the plaintiffs in Browder v. Gayle, the case whose ruling ultimately brought the boycott to an end.[71]

If we don't learn about those movement ancestors, we fall prey to exactly what James Baldwin warns us about. Ignoring them in favor of ambiguously heroic ancestors takes away our power. That power is one of the gifts that movement ancestors give us, whether we can trace our lineage back through bloodlines or not. We don't only belong to the people who sired us. We belong to the people

We don't only belong to the people who sired us. We belong to the people who fought for us before we even existed.

---

[71]https://lifeisasacredtext.substack.com/p/the-midwives-of-liberation   Read the whole thing!

who fought for us before we even existed. As Rabbi Rutenberg points out, even if they have been erased, they were there.

It's not surprising that this work is hard in different ways for white people than for people of color. In his insightful essay "Roots Deeper than Whiteness," David Dean writes:

> I am a descendant of some of the first Europeans to come to the land now known as the eastern United States. Their experiences were not included in the version of European history I was taught, one that glorifies the violent exploits of a small elite while leaving out the ways of life of the vast majority of our ancestors. Instead, their story resembles a similar pattern to those of many European immigrant groups that would come after them: one of people stripped of their rich ethnic identities and given a false racial identity that would turn many against their allies of color and increase their compliance with the corporate exploitation of workers and the planet.[72]

My friends at Crossroads Anti-Racism Organizing and Training taught me years ago that one of the costs of whiteness (and one of the ways white supremacy protects itself) is "historical amnesia," a lack of ability to connect the past with the present. That's certainly true in regard to the atrocious ancestors, and we all have our work to do there, but it's also true with movement ancestors. As David Dean points out, history is intentionally taught in the ways it is in order to diminish the odds of white people seeing more than one way of connecting with people of color, historically as well as today.

The Trump administration was a trying season for both activists and organizers, and for people with compassion for people who are oppressed, and for people who are oppressed. But it wasn't the only xenophobic era that had shaped me. I was born in Britain during a period of intense anti-Brown and anti-Black xenophobia. While watching the documentary

---

[72]"Roots Deeper than Whiteness: Remembering who we are for the well-being of all, By David Dean, used in the esteemed racial justice program for white people, White Awake. https://www.davidbfdean.com/roots-abridged?fbclid=IwAR0fu1B-BeoQbAD6wxz-GJnJv3vdnswlqnNfWE830xH-221b9ebvM48hkKs. Thanks to my friend Nichola Torbett who originally shared it with me and who does excellent work in this arena herself.

"White Riot" at the 3rd i Film Festival in 2021, I learned about the role that working-class musicians had in fighting back against fascism during that time. And understand, the time I'm talking about is when a prominent British politician's popular catch phrase was "Send 'em all back!"

This quote reminded me of the people who shaped the future that I inhabit as an activist, stated by one of the founders of Rockers Against Racism. "In this society, we're made to feel powerless and useless and that the great and the good should do our thinking for us. One of the wonderful things we were able to do in RAR was to say, 'No. Just ordinary people, we can do things. We can change the world.'"

While white supremacists marched through the streets of London in the 1970s waving British flags and Confederate flags, working-class youth of all races stood up against them and took down the white supremacists.

Knowing that that really happened, that it happened while my family were the ones navigating that racism, allowed me to imagine participating in a movement like that now, with regular people like you and me coming together and shutting down a political movement dedicated to erasing the people we love. I am so glad to know that working-class punks fought for baby Sandhya way back then. I want to channel their power in every way possible, in ways that honor who they were and how they resisted.

One of the major stumbling blocks for people connecting with any ancestors, including movement ancestors, is that although Christians sometimes talk about the cloud of saints, even the people who fought for justice were flawed. They were not necessarily saints, as we tend to think of them. Whether they were flawed because of their human finitude, because they had a little power and used it less than wisely or compassionately, or because they thought they could get away with it, they were not perfect. It is important to note that our need for our movement heroes/sheroes/theyroes to be perfect gets in the way of us connecting with them.

Earlier I mentioned Bhagat Singh Thind, who demanded US citizenship for South Asians in the Supreme Court in 1923. As it turns out, a lot of the Thind case's arguments were super racist against Black people.

Similarly, the movement ancestors in Bacon's Rebellion were brave and joined in common cause as Black enslaved people with white indentured servants, but they participated in violent attacks on Indigenous people.

When we only have the paradigms of saints and devils, we end up having very few ancestors to turn to. As a result, we might replicate the harm our ancestors both suffered and perpetuated. As we explored atrocious ancestors, we learned that people defy easy categories. There's another Christian tradition that echoes this: at the same time, we are always sinners and saints. Both/and.

But looking for perfect, sainted movement ancestors might not be the only option available to us. In fact, it's often said that "the perfect is the enemy of the good." I recently heard Rebecca Cokley, a prominent disability rights leader, on the radio show *The Takeaway,* and she illustrated this point beautifully.

She shared this interaction with Congressman John Lewis, about the complexity of our movement ancestors and what that offers us as possibilities today.

> Shortly following the Trump election, I found myself sitting in the Congressman's office. At the time, I was serving as the executive director of the National Council on Disability. The Congressman and I had a long storied, melded family history. I remember sitting there and saying to him, "Okay, Congressman, if anybody has any answer, if anybody can be our compass in this moment, it's you. What do we do now?"

> He started pointing to the photos on his wall, and to be in John Lewis's office was like sitting in the pages of the United States history book, except the photos on his wall, the same ones we saw in our books, were his personal photos. He pointed at one photo of a couple, and he said, "They were in an abusive relationship." He said, "We didn't say anything because the gentleman in the photo came from money, and his dad put a lot of money into the movement space, so we never said anything."

> He said, "I don't know what exactly happened to them." He pointed at another photo and said, "That's my friend. He went to Vietnam and came back physically but not psychologically. The last time I saw him, he was living homeless in Philadelphia." He

looked at me and said, "Rebecca, if there's anything that your generation can do differently than my generation, it's take care of your people."

As we have these conversations about the need to fund movements, about the need to bolster organizations, he said, "Don't ever lose sight of the fact that they don't exist without the people doing the work, and so check in with your people, hold them tight." I remember he said, "Be a phalanx where you can." He said, "They're going to try to find ways repeatedly to divide and conquer our people, and we just can't let that happen."[73]

One of the overwhelming complaints, frustrations, and heartbreaks I hear these days from longtime social justice organizers and activists is how impossible the standards are, and how short we always fall, and how quick people are to condemn.

Perhaps the gift of telling the full stories of our complex ancestors isn't only to stop romanticizing them. It's to help us show up for each other differently in the midst of our imperfect, human fullness and complexity. Perhaps our movement ancestors offer us both sources of inspiration and reminders of our limitations, both of which help us build power together differently and to love better.

My friend Cherri did me the great kindness of meeting with a community organizing class I was teaching early in 2022. She knew the class was all Black, and she brought the genius and spirit of Black ancestors into the classroom, knowing that I couldn't. She evoked the practice of sawubona,[74] the Zulu greeting that means "I see you." She quoted Fannie Lou Hamer, a powerful although overlooked ancestor of the US freedom movement, who once admonished people, "Never to forget where we came from and always praise the bridges that carried us over."[75]

Now, Fannie Lou Hamer is a source of inspiration to me. I have listened to the speech she made on the floor of the Democratic National

[73]https://www.wnycstudios.org/podcasts/takeaway/segments/how-hollywood-harms-dwarfism-community

[74]A Zulu greeting that translates to "I see you." (One response is "shiboka," "I exist for you.) This phrase has been increasingly embraced in Black activist spaces.

[74]For the full quote and more about Fannie Lou Hamer, visit the facebook page for the Alluvial Collective: https://www.facebook.com/AlluvialCollective/posts/

Convention in 1964 and been spurred to action. I absolutely consider her a movement ancestor.

But I can only do that with a clear sense that she offers me wisdom into what life was like for people whose struggles were different from my own people's, so that I can show up in solidarity. I can call on her as a movement ancestor only if I am clear that her work has much to teach me about how I do my own organizing work (deep relationship, lots of listening, community building, responding to people's immediate needs as well as casting a big enough vision), but her struggle was not my struggle.

In some ways, the way I relate to Fannie Lou Hamer or the Welsh miners or many of the movement ancestors here is not that different from the way I relate to my movement colleagues who are alive here today. It's appropriate to learn from them and to trade stories, to be inspired by the work that's happening in rural communities and on the South Side of Chicago and among Bhutanese refugees.

There are certainly times that I'll have gifts to offer folks organizing in those communities. And there are definitely times that they have wisdom that shapes my work. Our relationships work when they're grounded in respect and love and solidarity. But they don't work if I over-identify with their experiences, since their experiences and their terrain and their communities aren't mine.

It is also true that the gifts of Fannie Lou Hamer to the Black students in my organizing class addressing issues like water safety and housing justice and access to health care in the Black community are going to land differently for them than for me. But those Black students are also learning from other movement ancestors across historical lines, ancestors like Cesar Chavez and Gandhi and Gustavo Gutierrez and Filipino plantation workers. Those students are navigating the relationships to those ancestors across different contexts but make no mistake: those movement ancestors are helping shape their organizing projects, too.

My relationship to my movement ancestors is different than to my cultural or biological ancestors but no less essential in my work. I do not know where I would be or who I would be without them.

WHERE WE CAN GO FROM HERE

○ *If you want to write and reflect on this chapter's theme in your own life:*

Try to create a genealogy, except not a biological one: a movement genealogy. (I was inspired by Jesse Jackson who was inspired by MLK who was inspired by Gandhi who was inspired by Thoreau, etc. Or like in this chapter, The Fight for Fifteen was inspired by Occupy was inspired by Seattle WTO protests, and so on.)

○ *If you want to engage a personal ritual around this chapter's theme:*

Speaking a genealogy out loud is part of a lot of rituals to honor those who went before. Speak out loud your movement genealogy, laying down a flower or seed at an altar, at your bedside, wherever is a special place for you. "I am ____, child of _____, son of _____," etc., until you've gone down at least seven levels.

○ *If you want to engage your activist or spiritual group in a practice that will help them begin to connect with ancestors in new ways as part of their work to dismantle white supremacy:*

Each of you name a movement ancestor. See if you can find ways that the movements they were a part of connected with each other. Consider representing this on a whiteboard, with lines that connect various movements (abolition and suffrage, for example).

Chapter Eight

Spiritual Ancestors

Our religion is the traditions of our ancestors - the dreams of our old men, given them in solemn hours of the night by the Great Spirit; and the visions of our sachems, and is written in the hearts of our people.

—Chief Seattle

I feel like every time Handel's *Messiah* is played each December, a little piece of a Jewish ancestor dies. I mean, that's not how I understand ancestors, but you know what I'm getting at. One of the most beautiful compositions in the western canon, the songs pull largely from the book of Isaiah, a book written by and for Jewish ancestors navigating an era of conquest and exile and turns those words into a prediction of the coming Jesus Christ.

Of course it does. How could it be otherwise?

Handel was writing during an era of Christian supremacy, and he was taught that the only reason the Jewish Bible existed was to predict the coming of Jesus, or at least that any reference to a Messiah in the Jewish Bible was a prediction of the coming of Jesus. In the process, he and all the Christians who practiced this belief (called *supersessionism*) missed out on what those spiritual ancestors might actually have been saying.

What's tricky about spiritual ancestors—the ancestors who emerge from our current religious traditions or the traditions of our ancestors—is that often we have been taught to ignore their context when their context shaped their experiences as much as our context shapes ours. Yet if we listen to them in their own contexts, they have so much wisdom to offer us in ours. They have so much more to offer than many of us have been allowed to imagine.

Different from cultural and movement ancestors and yet deeply entwined and sometimes overlapping with both, how do we engage the ancestors from our various spiritual traditions? How do we learn from what they did that contributed to liberation? How do we listen for the suppressed stories of liberation between the lines? How do we pay attention to the fact that for some of us, those ancestors had their own cultural and political context different from our own?

I think a lot about the fact that while Robert the Bruce, King of Scotland, was a practicing and faithful Christian, he turned to the Celtic priests when his battle against the English seemed unwinnable. And while those Celtic priests had to follow their druidic (non-Christian) practices in secret due to the dominance of Christianity, it was their blessing that made him believe the Scots could actually win against the English. Even Robert the Bruce's spiritual ancestry was more diverse than you'd think!

By this point in the book, you already know my guiding theory about spiritual ancestors. It's the same as my theory about other ancestors: the liberative ones have often been kept from us, and the "well-behaved ones" get trotted out instead. (Even though we all know the saying: well-behaved ancestors rarely made history.)

I had conversations with Black and Asian American Christians about this book who were so excited that I was exploring ancestors because they had been told that it was demonic to be connected to the spiritual practices of their (non-Christian) ancestors.

In one of the people of color wisdom circles that contributed to this book, a friend of mine from the Muslim tradition said, "The story of Lilith has been erased." It turns out she has delved deeply into the story of Lilith, in some traditions believed to be the first woman in the Jewish Bible. Lilith is said to have been written out because she was too strong and too committed to her own worth as equal to Adam. Her life redacted, she is replaced in the subsequent, remaining narrative by Eve, who is described as a helpmeet to Adam instead of his equal.

One of the most famous Hindu stories is the Ramayana, which follows the tale of the demon king Ravana who kidnaps the god Ram's wife Sita. The story goes that when Ram finally rescues her, he worries that her virtue has been tainted by Ravana, so he has her walk through a purifying fire that, if she has been defiled, will destroy her. She unhesitatingly walks through the fire to confirm for her god and husband that she remains pure. I hate this story with my own kind of purifying fire, and I'm not the only one. The 1996 Deepa Mehta film takes on this story through a queer love story and many others have wrestled with this text over the years.

We're not always encouraged to encounter our spiritual ancestors in any terms other than the ones our community has decided are acceptable, much the way we don't get to encounter our biological ancestors except in the ways they've been mediated for us by our ancestors. When it comes to the Ramayana, it's been around long enough that it's bound to have been interpreted and reinterpreted.

So, what does it look like for us to build up a practice of engaging spiritual ancestors and their stories in new ways? Not just as artists or filmmakers, but as descendants seeking wisdom and relationship. What might that open up? How do we listen for stories that honor them, seek practices that do the same, while casting aside that which is oppressive or harmful?

Seeking to find spiritual wisdom within this frustrating story, I find that now I imagine Sita going into the fire, not to prove her purity to Ram, but as an act of resistance. "I was kidnapped for over a year by a demon god, and your biggest concern is whether I'm pure enough? If I had been raped, you wouldn't want me anymore? Fine. I'll walk across this fire; whether I burn or whether the flames turn to lotuses, may it bring you shame."

If we listen well, what surprising things will we hear our spiritual ancestors tell us?

Bill Keegan, an archaeologist with the Florida Museum of Natural History, created a four-minute video of the origins of the world from the perspective of the Taino people, a highly advanced Indigenous people who thrived for the thousand years before the European colonization of the Americas.[76] He made clear that these origin stories were not intended for literal interpretation but as an emotional journey.

That origin story told of four brothers forced from the world of the divine onto our earth. The fourth brother had scars and wounds and physical afflictions he didn't understand until someone spit tobacco on him, causing a sore on his back to swell until his brothers thought he would die. When they cut open the sore, out swam a turtle who could travel gracefully on both land and water. With this, the brother understood his role as the connection between this earth and the earth of the sacred, beginning a tradition of people with various physical challenges being recognized as having this connection between worlds.

Perhaps it's because none of my ancestors are Taino, but hearing that story and not needing it to align with my worldview gave me a chance to see how a different community made sense of a global issue in a particular way. My Christian and Jewish friends are constantly having to work against religious texts that often seem to treat physical, emotional, and mental disabilities as a result of sin.

Our spiritual ancestors offer us wisdom about how to navigate the challenges of our lives and how to hold onto hope in the face of adversity. When we can take a step back, though, they might also offer us insight into why we see things the way we do. If we are given the special gift of learning about one another's spiritual ancestors, we might gain insights into our worldview's limitations or fall more deeply in love with our own.

My friend, Fiza, who has done so much research into Lilith, notes that in order to connect with her spiritual ancestors, she does two things in particular: she learns from primary sources more than from interpretations, and she focuses on being a listener when she reads.

Fiza makes that sound easy. But listening to ancestors in the ancient texts means doing a lot of things. In addition to developing an ear for an ancient style of writing, it means listening to what her ancestors were going through when this was written, listening for who got to do the writing and who didn't. It means, as Wendy Doniger suggests, listening for what made it into the text even though it was countercultural for the time and for what the text over emphatically refutes because it's trying to

---

[76]https://www.floridamuseum.ufl.edu/science/taino-origin-story/?fbclid=I-wAR14WFVpYaIM1_uNY83w9OQVs9r5XT59jCt1Gcitn1mcJPEk6yLsVDHZGlQ

quash a nascent uprising. So, when Fiza reads Genesis 1 from the Jewish Bible, she's more likely than most of us to notice there are actually two different versions of the creation story in that chapter, back-to-back, and that in the first one, man and woman are created simultaneously and equally in the image of God, whereas in the second one, man comes first and then woman is created from man. That conflict of stories sends her down a road to learning about that first woman, Fiza's spiritual ancestor Lilith, and the many stories about her.

In one of the white people's wisdom circles that shaped this book, my friend Cathy reflected on some powerful spiritual ancestors in their Unitarian tradition, a tradition I have been guilty of painting as all one thing because I haven't been exposed to its ancestors. Cathy told us about the role of Unitarians in the Hungarian Resistance and the long pro-worker and pro-women history of the Waldenses in Italy, a pre-Reformation ascetic and pacifist group that challenged corruption in the church and continues to practice to this day. In simply asking a question about the spiritual ancestors who brought stories of resistance, I ended up being blessed by ancestors I did not know and now wanted to learn from.

In that same conversation, we talked also about how prior to the witch hunts, magic and connection to nature had simply existed as part of the world, and it was only when poor people resisted their mistreatment did magic become a threat and incompatible with Christianity. One of the participants grieved how often she heard people say, "I'm not into church but nature," and how sad those things are seen as incompatible. She wanted to honor her ancestors, the ones then demonized as witches, who had seen church and nature as inextricably bound together, the same ancestors whose minimal amount of freedom was so threatening that they were deemed demonic.

In the most heartbreaking part of the conversation, someone asked, "How do I unpack this connection to a rigid church invested in the state and in policing when we're talking about spiritual ancestors who were killed for seeing the church differently than that?" At the same time, everyone in the group knew that was why we had gathered: our current experiences of our cultural communities were misaligned with what some of our spiritual ancestors had sought to create.

Within the Storytelling Project Model, this whole section lives solidly in the Resistance stories. And while many of my activist colleagues have given up on spirituality or religion altogether, some of us feel a connection to the divine or the universe or oneness that opens up opportunities for us to connect with spiritual ancestors and with some sacred mystery well beyond us.

In the past five to ten years, there have been numerous articles written about people of color in the US leaving Christianity and returning to the religious traditions of their ancestors instead; people like NoNo, a Salvadoran person of Mayan descent who grew up in LA and identifies as a *Bruja* (a Spanish word for witch or sorceress, similar to the Celtic *brixta*, which means magic). "[For me], you can be a bruja from Africa, from an Indigenous background, an Asian bruja, a f***ing European Viking. There's just a lot of ways that someone can identify as a witch or a healer or as a person that's tapped [into spirituality]."[77] Part of the power of these connections is that they resonate with our culture. Part is that they resonate with our spirit. Part is that they connect us to something removed from colonization.

That last sentence is complicated. As part of the South Asian community, I'm aware of what missionaries did to undermine Indian autonomy and how they used religion as one tool to achieve that. I have a Fijian Indian friend who converted from Christianity, the religion of her ancestors' colonizers, to her ancestral Hinduism.

I also have numerous friends whose ancestors converted to Christianity as Dalits to choose a religion free from caste. (Buddhism, Islam, and Sikhism likewise have received converts for similar reasons.) I already mentioned my passion for Hindu liberation theology in response to some friends determining that Hinduism was "uniquely irredeemable" in the face of its origins in Brahminical patriarchy.

The reality, I imagine, is that many of us connecting with ancestral religions bump into similar problems if we engage deeply enough— histories of violence, patriarchy and misogyny, tribalism, and other practices that do not align with who we seek to be today.

Perhaps that is also part of why connecting with spiritual ancestors is so important, whether it is as we reconnect with the rituals and practices of our ancestors, or as a way of understanding them in their fullness and complexity.

---

[77]https://www.vice.com/en/article/qvwe3x/the-young-brujas-reclaiming-the-power-of-their-ancestors

I am an ordained Christian minister. My Hindu family in India know that and saw no conflict between that and their expectation that I play a role in chanting the Sanskrit verses and pouring the flowers and ghee and other sacred items over the box of my father's ashes before we placed them in the Ganges River so he might reach moksha and leave the cycle of reincarnation. I had no idea what the words meant, and no one, including the priest feeding me the lines, thought that mattered. What mattered was I was honoring my father the same way they had honored their father and mother, the same way my father had honored his grandmother when he was ten years old because his father couldn't reach the burning ghat[78] due to communal unrest in the region. The same way generations in my family have honored those who came before them. A whole lot of things have changed that a half-white unmarried Christian woman ended up being the one to make sure those ashes made it home. I never heard a person in the family suggest that it was anything other than sacred and honoring of our shared ancestors. In fact, I suspect they actually put in a lot of work to make sure I got to be part of the ceremony instead of my eldest male cousin doing the ritual with the priest while I watched.

One of my most beloved friends, more of a sister, is Patricia. We met through worker justice organizing, she served on the board of the Oakland Peace Center, and we have been friends for a decade. A big part of our relationship has to do with how our spirituality connects with our culture and with how we organize in community.

Since both of our fathers passed away, we've also talked about how we connect with the spirits and souls of the people who came before us for the sake of their healing and ours. Patricia plays an active role in the interfaith, Indigenous-led sweat lodge in which she is involved in Oakland. As I write this, she's on what I think of as a spiritual reunification tour in her homeland of Michoacan in Mexico. She is being reunified with her people, her ancestors, and with the land to which she belongs. Patricia introduced me to the work of Nick

[78]Burning ghats are places near the river designated for cremation

Estes—both to the podcast he co-hosts called *Red Nation* and to his book *Our History is the Future*, in which he shows how, in the eyes of Indigenous ancestors, the sharp lines drawn between politics, culture, and spirit were a lie.

By connecting with the practices of our ancestors and sharing those with each other, Patricia and I end up doing our organizing in ways that position us more powerfully, more relationally, and in a more spiritually grounded way. Before Patricia began her spiritual reunification tour, she and I met by the water in Oakland, shared stories to remember our people, and thanked the water and the spirit it holds, knowing that water has been a sacred portal for her people and mine and that water could hold our friendship and could hold her journey and could hold her ancestors—healers and those in need of healing alike.

Patricia and I found some of our own healing together, but what are we to do when it is our ancestors who are in need of spiritual healing?

In May of 2021, not long before he died, Thich Nhat Hanh, the famous Vietnamese Buddhist monk and peace activist, wrote a reflection on the wounded child within us and our need to tend to her. Here is his distinctly Buddhist way of engaging ancestral trauma through this metaphor:

> With practice, we can see that our wounded child is not only us. Our wounded child may represent several generations. Our mother may have suffered throughout her life. Our father may have suffered. Perhaps our parents weren't able to look after the wounded child in themselves. So, when we're embracing the wounded child in us, we're embracing all the wounded children of our past generations. This practice is not a practice for ourselves alone, but for numberless generations of ancestors and descendants.
>
> Our ancestors may not have known how to care for their wounded child within, so they transmitted their wounded child to us. Our practice is to end this cycle. If we can heal our wounded child, we will not only liberate ourselves, but we will also help liberate whoever has hurt or abused us. The abuser may also have been the victim of abuse. There are people who have practiced with their inner child for a long time who have had a lessening of their suffering and have experienced

transformation. Their relationships with their family and friends have become much easier.[79]

Across the globe from Thich Nhat Hanh's home in Plum Village, I was preaching at a church in a town I'll just refer to as "The Raisin Capital of the World," to keep the theme of locales named for fruits going a little longer. Folks from there know where I'm talking about.

My friend Charlotte was the worship leader that morning, and as she stood at the lectern, she said to the congregation, "Some of you know my grandfather left this church because of women being allowed to become elders [prominent lay leaders who preside over communion, a sacred part of the church's remembrance of Jesus' last meal with his Disciples]. Today after church," she said, choking down the emotion in her voice, "I'll be going to my first meeting as an elder of this church." She paused and then said in a loud, confident voice, "And he would not be upset about this!"

When I caught up with her after worship, I told her how much I loved that story because of this idea I've been sitting with that our ancestors can continue to heal, that these twenty or sixty or a hundred years we have on this earth are not our only shot to get it right (or that we keep having to work at it, lifetime after lifetime before reaching nirvana). She shared that her mother is navigating advanced dementia. The night before worship, Charlotte was checking with her dad to make sure she had the details of her grandfather's exit right. She said, "Wow, he really did leave because of women elders, and now I'm becoming a woman elder in that same church."

At that moment, her mother chimed in, "And he would not be upset about this!"

It was an unusually alert statement given her condition. Charlotte said when she talked with a friend about it later, her friend said sagely, "That was your grandfather speaking through her." So, to Charlotte's mind, ancestors can continue to heal.

---

[79]"Thich Nhat Hanh on Healing the Child Within," BY THICH NHAT HANH, Lion's Roar, MAY 19, 2021

There are ways we connect with spiritual ancestors in very different ways than those before us might have, or we get to connect with them more publicly because of the work our ancestors have done. I know that most Hindus don't think the trans figures in the Hindu texts automatically mean Hinduism should be trans friendly.

But you know who does encounter those trans spiritual ancestors as a source of support? Some trans Hindus.

In my research for the writing project about queer South Asian American ancestors, I came across a number of queer and trans figures in Hindu texts, including Shikandi. While I'm not Hindu, Shikandi speaks to the part of me that experiences gender binaries as harmful to who I am in the world and also finds them harmful to how we relate to a God who encompasses all genders. In that video essay, which was framed around the themes of ancestors and longing, I wrote:

> I don't think my longing is unusual. I think I long to be seen and accepted, an almost universal longing. When I don't experience being seen and accepted, it is comforting to know that amongst the hundreds of thousands of gods of my ancestors, there is one both universally loved and yet weaponized. Most Hindus know the story of Shikandi, born as a girl but raised as a boy, who transformed into a man on his wedding night. They know and celebrate Shikandi as a great warrior. Yet Shikandi is also an insult thrown at a mannish woman or an effeminate man. God, goddess, warrior, and still somehow inappropriate all at once. And one more adjective: unapologetic. As I look to ancestors, as I look for connection, I wonder if Shikandi can make that trek across the ocean for all of us who are in between, not enough and too much, to keep us company and help us transcend longing. I wonder if Shikandi and Mae Chung and Rose Bamberger and the founders of Shamakami are the ancestors of belonging to chase away the demons of longing.

Iya Funlayo E. Wood-Menzies is the founder of the Ase Ire Orisa temple, a spiritual community that is grounded in the African tradition of Ifa-Orisa. In one reflection on the temple's blog, Dr. Wood-Menzies noted that one of her Christian ancestors had pointed her to some important wisdom from the Bible, found in Psalm 58, about the pain that would befall oppressors and the comfort that the oppressed would receive. After offering an interpretation of this scripture and how it could be useful to her community, she noted:

> Although I don't incorporate Christian imagery into my practice of Ifá-Òrìsà tradition, I do keep some Christian items in my Egun space because, as a child of the Diaspora, I pay homage to my many ancestors who were Christian and provide items, like the Bible, that they can use to direct me in their own way. My Egun space is a space for my ancestral spirits to gather, it is their place, not mine, and I keep these items there in their honor.[80]

We might be at a point where we should (and you might very well only have bought this book in order to) talk seriously about ancestors having agency. This is where I begin to get outside my comfort zone although friends of mine have built houses and dwell in this space.

Some of my friends who are more at home in this part of their spiritual life are clear that if you do enough to open up your heart, you may receive real, palpable, worded wisdom from spiritual ancestors, be they Celtic or Orisha or Indigenous. They may help you see things about yourself that you can't see. They aren't necessarily just imagined beings we extrapolate from what we know of history. I have friends who have communicated with saints or ancestors, sometimes directly, sometimes through an intermediary.

I have very little to offer to that conversation other than to say if you want to explore that and know people who are that way gifted, ask them for their wisdom.

Increasingly, I know of people who have been returning to ancestral pre-Christian practices as a way to connect with their ancestors or their spirituality. This turn can be complicated. Sometimes those "ancestral pre-Christian practices," especially those from Nordic cultures, are used to justify white supremacy. Sometimes we have to come to terms with the knowledge that our spiritual ancestors engaged in harmful practices and beliefs alongside the ones we'd like to emulate. Sometimes, maybe even often, people engage ancient practice in colonizing or appropriative ways.

---

[80] 25 Mar Messages From Egun (Ancestors): Psalms 58, https://aseire.com/2019/03/25/messages-from-egun-ancestors-psalms-58

Tatianna Morales, who comes from Puerto Rican ancestors, lives in New Orleans and is best known as "Tatianna Tarot" on Instagram, offers some helpful wisdom in relation to that issue:

> For whatever reason right now, brujas are really trendy. And I think that there's pros and cons to that. Like, hell yeah! Ideally, we are really all brujas and brujos. My definition [of a bruja] is honing in on your personal power and working with the energies around you to create the life that you want. So ultimately, we all are capable of that. But it's important to know that people have been doing it way before we have been doing it. It's important to know and respect that knowledge, those people, and where it came from.[81]

· · · · · · · · · · · · · · · · · · · ·

"[Brujería] is in our blood and must be activated for our empowerment and for the abolishment of the patriarchal rule."
— Tatianna Morales

Because you know by now that I do not see the work of connecting with ancestors as simply personal work, you won't be surprised that my favorite reflection from Morales on this subject is this little add-on: "[Brujería] is in our blood and must be activated for our empowerment and for the abolishment of the patriarchal rule. Reclaiming brujería is reclaiming our story and finding our voice as divine beings again."

Our spiritual ancestors are sometimes our cultural ancestors and sometimes our political ancestors. That intersection gets ignored far too often, especially for those of us in religious traditions where the people at the top want to make sure things stay the way they are.

※※※※※ ※※※※※

For many of the people I wrote about in this chapter, turning to ancestral, usually pre-Christian, pre-colonization, religion has helped free them from the ways religion can oppress. For others, recognizing the dissenting voices within their tradition connects them to the ancestors they need.

---

[81]https://www.vice.com/en/article/qvwe3x/the-young-brujas-reclaiming-the-power-of-their-ancestors

One such illustration is found in an excruciatingly good essay written by Grace Park for *Inheritance Magazine* in 2020. While Park has not rejected Korean Christianity, she has found her people and her resistance movement within it in the midst of a sacred, traditional Korean Christian celebration. While I can't share the entire essay, let me share one passage that points out how it is an impossible and maybe unnecessary task for us to separate out the cultural and spiritual and movement ancestors. Having quoted the 강강술래 (ganggangsullae) at the beginning of her essay (a mother offering to sell the rice paddy so her daughter can have shoes or sell the farm so her daughter can have a servant and her daughter saying she doesn't need those things from her mother), she comes back to it mid-essay:

> 추석 is more than just a celebration of anticipation or supplication to deities and ancestors. It is not about wishful thinking or spiritual bypassing that temporarily distances ourselves from our bodily experiences and the physical world. Rather, 추석 celebration must be deeply rooted in and manifest through our bodies.
>
> So, I turn to the 강강술래 (ganggangsullae).
>
> We have been told that it originated from village folks celebrating the full moon's light, highest around the time of the autumn harvest, to bring about a bountiful harvest once more. But if you listened more closely, you would realize that the women, for it has most always been women in the 강강술래, were also singing their hopes and desires for themselves and each other, venting their frustrations, their pain from the hard labor and mistreatment they experienced as working-class women, as women in a deeply patriarchal society that did not allow them to sing loudly, to dance passionately, to go outside at night, to have their bodies as their own.[82]

The best of our spiritual ancestors fought for our connection to the sacred around us and within us. They sought to protect us for the sake of being better community to one another. They preserved stories of liberation that those with power sought to take away from us. They

---

[82]but you CAN read it here: https://www.inheritancemag.com/stories/chuseok

exist within every spiritual tradition. May we find them. May we share them. May we one day be them.

WHERE WE CAN GO FROM HERE

○ *If you want to write and reflect on this chapter's theme in your own life:*

Think about a value that is incredibly important to you. Write about someone from your spiritual heritage who embodied that value, and how they practiced it. Write about how their practice connects to yours, or how it inspires yours.

○ *If you want to engage a personal ritual around this chapter's theme:*

What is the way your spiritual tradition honors those who have passed? From All Souls' Day to Dia de los Muertos to Samhain and more, our traditions often have specific rituals we use to honor the dead, including things like the pouring of libations or setting up an altar. Look around and see which process comes from your tradition. Engage in it.

○ *If you want to engage your activist or spiritual group in a practice that will help them begin to connect with ancestors in new ways as part of their work to dismantle white supremacy:*

Share with each other a meditation or prayer practice that you like, and where it comes from—its history and heritage, and why it speaks to you. Offer to try one or two with each other.

SECTION III: How to integrate our ancestors

As we move into this phase, we consider the emerging/ transforming stories of both our colleagues and ourselves and eventually move towards action and change.

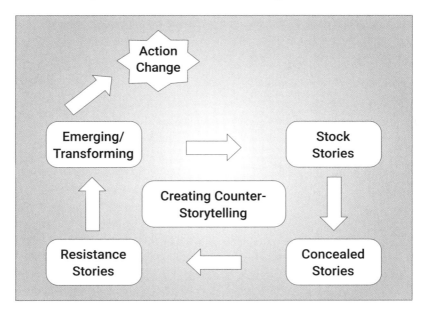

Chapter Nine

Landscape Ancestors

In 1881, my dad's grandparents, who were Norwegian farmers, immigrated to the United States - the same year my great grandfather from Laguna Pueblo was put on a train to Carlisle Indian School in Pennsylvania.

—Deb Haaland

I was driving down the 101, a highway in the farm country of central California, when I noticed a different sign than the ones I've noticed before. The historic marker signs I remember on that stretch of highway are still there, and they read "Calle Real," Royal Highway, a marker of the Spanish colonial missions that brutalized Indigenous people beginning in 1769. This time, though, I saw a new sign as well: "Bracero Memorial Highway." That sign remembered the guest workers who worked that land for decades, some of whose descendants still work the land and a handful of whose descendants even own the land or the trucks that ship food across country or who got degrees and are doctors and teachers and accountants, and some of whose descendants returned to Mexico to do all those same things.

It was a sign that made me pause and reflect on the landscape through which I was driving, and whose land it actually was, and who had lived and loved and lost on that land. Like I said, I've driven that highway before, and when I saw the sign "King's Highway," I thought for a little bit about the Spanish king who never set foot here, but mostly it just got me singing my favorite gospel song. This time, reading "Bracero Memorial Highway," I found myself thinking of the land and whose lives were shaped by it.

You and I and the people we know here in the US have ancestors who came by force, left by force, came to conquer, came to seek out a better life. All their stories intertwine with each other and shape our relationship to the land today. We live on this land, but most of us are not of it. What does it mean for us to listen to the ancestors of this land? How do those ancestors shape the way we engage each other and the land itself?

In an earlier chapter, I wrote of my experience of an "aboriginal walkabout" tour of the Blue Mountains and how our guide shared that while he was from another part of Australia, their tradition was to identify with the Indigenous people of the land on which they lived. It's been fifteen years since I heard him say that, and his words have never left me because they point to a different relationship to land than I have. I am so moved by this notion that I would claim and be claimed by the people on whose land I live. The only way to think like that, I imagine, is to have completely released the idea that land can or should be commodified. In other words, I would need to let go of the idea that individual or corporate ownership of land is real or appropriate.

You may have heard people marvel at the myth of how Manhattan was traded for a handful of beads. I remember learning about that in elementary school and the kids in class thinking how bad at trading or how dumb the Manhasset were. But the error didn't lie with the Manhasset. If the European colonizers had understood that the land wasn't supposed to be a commodity, perhaps they could have learned to work the land together. Perhaps they could have engaged each other constructively. Perhaps the violence and bloodshed and genocide would not have been deemed necessary, all for the purpose of taking land. If they had understood the land as the Manhasset did, we would be living in a very different world today.

There's a quote from the Palestinian poet Mourid Bhargouti that I first learned from the famous "Danger of the Single Story" TED Talk by Chimamanda Adichie. Bhargouti says, "If you want to dispossess a people, start by telling their story, and begin with secondly."

I quote this line so often that people I love remember me saying it.

If you've never heard the talk, you might wonder what Bhargouti means. He means that the people with the power tell the story, and they tell it in ways that erase their culpability and highlight the injustices they have endured, removing the idea that these "injustices" might have been consequences rather than completely out of the blue.

Once, a colleague of mine showed up at a staff meeting and said, "Sandhya, you were right with that whole 'begin with secondly' thing!" She and her boyfriend had gone hiking in Yosemite National Park that weekend, and while reading one of the historical placards, they noted that one said, "Yosemite Valley was discovered by white settlers after being driven into it by surrounding Native people," or words to that effect. (I imagine that placard no longer exists; the park underwent a significant re-branding around 2018 to eliminate inappropriate misuse of Indigenous names and stories.) It was the perfect illustration of "beginning with secondly." If you begin with secondly, you end up with settlers "discovering" something that clearly the Indigenous people already knew about. If you begin with secondly, you end up with settlers being "driven" into the valley instead of the settlers trespassing on Indigenous land in the first place.

For too long, the stories of those ancestors with the most power have begun with "secondly." How do we turn that on its head? And how might it create healing to start with "first" instead? Would we see our own healing, or healing of the land, or of our ancestors?

⊰⊰⊰⊰⊰⊰ ⊱⊱⊱⊱⊱⊱

Sinéad Talley, who is Karuk and Yurok,[83] has been on her own journey related to self-understanding as an Indigenous person. "It's taken a long time for me to get outside of the blood quantum construct of thinking," says Talley.

> I'm low blood quantum, and my family was disconnected for a while before we came back to the river. It's been a returning process.
>
> Learning more about history and the fact that blood quantum is a European concept and not how Native people determined

---

[83]Karuk and Yoruk are Indigenous tribes in California.

who was a community member and who was not helped. When it comes down to it, blood quantum doesn't mean anything. [Rather] it's your connection to place, it's your kinship ties and how involved you are in the community. It has a lot to do with a lot of things, but Indigeneity doesn't have to do with blood quantum. You can know that and you can feel that, but they're two different things. For me it's taken a long time to feel that.[84]

In some ways, Talley is pointing to a vision akin to that of the tour guide on the Aboriginal walkabout, that we are called to connect to the land, the community on the land, and the ancestors of the land.

I think that connection to a particular place can be a way we connect to ancestors (and so can food). But for those of us who do not live on the land of our ancestors, we have some discerning to do about how we choose to relate to the ancestors on whose land we live, and it's often not a choice many of us realize we have already made.

My friend Bentley shared with me this quote from Douglas John Hall on "the peculiar brand of theological triumphalism that came to be in American Christianity."

It is worth contemplating whether the superficial hold on the life of this continent that . . . Christianity has been able to achieve, is in some mysterious way related to its missionary refusal to enter humbly into the life of the land's own peoples and to respect the gods of the land. Autochthonous [Indigenous] religion should never be lightly brushed aside, for it is the deepest expression of the relationship between humanity and the world of nature and spirit that has been acquired by centuries of love and suffering in that place. As such it contains wisdom that cannot be imported from elsewhere. Perhaps we are just now seeing the terrible consequences of the noncontextual, European conquest of a continent whose gods have been deeply offended by the emissaries of a foreign deity.[85]

---

[84]"I'm Dreaming About a Modern World That Doesn't Erase Its Indigenous Intelligence," Matika Wilbur, *Yes* magazine, Spring 2018, https://www.yesmagazine. org/issue/decolonize/2018/02/19/im-dreaming-about-a-modern-world-that-do esnt-erase-its-indigenous-intelligence?fbclid=IwAR2xDly20PILSgJ_B2_KcDlCy5fl-TlTrJ8w9NwteMsEXSc1oiz0pXxxuumY

[85]Douglas, John Hall. Professing the Faith: Christian Theology in a North American Context. 1996; Fortress Press. P. 111.

I've mentioned before a presentation Indigenous activist Mark Charles gave to a predominantly (but not entirely) white audience at a prominent church in Berkeley. (Shout out to Project Peace East Bay for organizing it and for making sure that local Indigenous organizer Corrina Gould played a key role.) During that presentation he said something very similar to something I've heard Corrina say as well. He said he was tired of how all people ever say about Native people is how tragic their story is, when in fact Indigenous people are not only victims, they have so much to offer and to teach. The way Corrina says it is, "We're not victims. We're hosts."

That day Charles also talked about how it was a little like Indigenous people owned a house, and then a bunch of people moved into the house, and at first the owners were like, "ummm, OK, we'll make room for you. That's our values." But at a certain point the owners were like, "OK, you're not treating our home with any respect. You've gotta go."

They even pulled out their baseball bats to show they meant business. But by now, there were a *lot* of visitors, and they were armed with guns, and they killed off some of the owners' family, and they pushed the owners into one little bedroom upstairs while they threw a decade-long rager in the rest of the house. Now, suddenly, the guests are coming into the little bedroom and saying "we love you, owners of this house. Teach us your ways." But the owners are old now, and tired, and can't get down the stairs anymore.

I remember hearing Charles and Gould talk about their relationship to the land and their relationship to non-Indigenous people (primarily white people) that night and I had a huge awakening that I'm not sure anyone I've shared it with has found to be quite as profound as I did. I'm going to share it anyhow, because it has tilted my world a little to the side.

My family moved to this country in 1978. The company my father worked for helped us pursue US citizenship, and within five years, we were being sworn in.

At no point in that journey to citizenship did we ever knowingly encounter Indigenous people, seek their permission or wisdom, or engage anyone but the governmental descendants of an occupying force in order to become part of this country. I was maybe twenty-five before I encountered a self-identifying Indigenous person. I had been a citizen for eighteen years by then. If I didn't know living Indigenous people, I

definitely wasn't in conversation with Indigenous ancestors on the land
I lived on in Akron or Chicago or Baltimore or Oakland. And if I wasn't
in conversation with the ancestors of those pieces of land, I was not in
conversation with the land itself.

It is critical, I am finally learning, to hone those relationships in order
to be in right relationship with the land. Over time, we might learn of
healing work that is ours to do, or reparations or restitution. There is
much to grieve, in fact, as we come to terms with the disconnect so many
of us have from ancestors of this land.

If you are not of Indigenous ancestry (or you are, but you're not in touch
with the land or the ancestors where you currently live) and are feeling
a little despondent at this point, I want to share with you one of the most
inspiring challenges I've received in recent years.

In 2018, I attended an event for a labor justice organization where I
currently serve on the board, and my colleague Patricia St. Onge brought
the opening spiritual grounding for the event. Pat is Indigenous and grew
up in New England. She works hard to be in active relationship with the
diverse array of Indigenous people in the Bay Area of California, including
the original people of the land, the confederated Ohlone people.

"Everyone in this room
at one point came from
people who didn't just
believe that the land
belonged to them, but
who understood *that they
belonged to the land.*"
— Patricia St. Onge

People attended this event for
a number of different reasons
though most came because they
care about unions and workers.
While some of them also cared
about the intersections of worker
justice, eco-justice and Indigenous
solidarity, many did not. As part
of her opening blessing, Patricia
said to the hundreds gathered,
"Everyone in this room at one
point came from people who
didn't just believe that the land belonged to them, but who understood
that *they belonged to the land.*" She invited all of us to get in touch with
our own ancestors (indigenous to places all over the globe) to reconnect
with that type of relationship to the land.

It was such an elegant turn of phrase and it also demanded something of me that I carried with me when I took my father's ashes back to India. I shared her words with the women of my family who translated it into Bengali for each other. I explained that this issue was at the heart of the ancestors book I was writing. It resonated in each of their hearts as well. They agreed and said this was the way people can find peace.

And yet. The land they saw themselves belonging to was in the town of Malda, a bigger town where they've lived for the past forty or so years, or the village of Sovanagar, where my father went to primary school and lived with his father's mother. We have maybe a hundred years of family history there.

They didn't see themselves belonging to the village of Tildanga where we still own an acre of rice paddy. It was to Tildanga that my father still felt he belonged.

Tildanga is a village of maybe 500, and people don't usually leave. If they do, it is not usually to go to other states or countries. It is an 80 percent Muslim village, and my family was the only Brahmin family in the village when my father was growing up. I know this because on a visit to the village, I got to meet one of the oldest couples in the village. My cousins were so excited for me to meet the wife because she has tattoos tying her to her ancestry. I'm the only person in my family with them (and the only one in my generation with a nose ring, although my eldest sister-in-law used to have one before they lost their worth as a status symbol).

The wife told me (through my nieces' translation) that she remembered my grandfather. He had performed their wedding. Remember, Brahmin is a caste status *and* it originated as a demarcation of who was allowed to be a priest. My grandfather wasn't a priest. He had the equivalent of an eighth-grade education. But that meant he was the most highly educated in the village and therefore headmaster of the village school. In the absence of any practicing priests, my grandfather met the basic requirements as the only male Brahmin who had gone through the coming-of-age ceremony.

Still abuzz with a romantic version of Pat's message about belonging to the land and finally back on the family compound that had shaped everyone in my generation except me, I asked the woman, "Have you ever thought of living anywhere besides Tildanga?" She responded with the sweetest smile I could imagine. "Where would we go?" she asked. "This is home."

Now the way I wrote that sounds so wholesome and confirming of what I had gone to India looking for. But I know enough about non-verbal communication that I realized her statement wasn't out of a stereotypical Hindi film with a happy ending. It was out of a tragic Bengali film, in which a young bride full of hope realizes she will never get to leave the confines of a small village that offers no hope of a better life than was available to the generation before her.

I also got to spend a little time with the man who takes care of our acre of rice paddy and who keeps our ancestral compound locked up and maintained. His father did the same before him. His father is the person who taught my father and uncle and cousins the practical aspects of their relation to the land, and as a result of that training, my father was a lifelong gardener with a deep love of helping food emerge from whichever plot of earth he was on.

I asked the caretaker of our land and his best friend about any religious practices that felt particular to them in their region, and they talked about how they stood in a particular way during prayers at their mosque, while at the mosque in the next village people positioned their feet differently, and it was interesting to note these small distinctions from one community to the next. I also asked him if he ever thought of living anywhere else. He gave me the same answer as the woman from the oldest couple in the village, shyly, a little hangdog, "Where would we go? This is home."

I was reminded in those conversations that our relationships to the land are not necessarily less complicated than our relationships to our other ancestors. I was also reminded that throughout our history my family got to move, and we got to move to land we owned. We had the privilege of choosing the places we considered ours. Our relationship to the land might be as complicated as anyone else's, but our feelings about that land were surely less ambivalent.

"Everyone in this room at one point came from people who didn't just believe that the land belonged to them, but who understood that *they belonged to the land.*"

Pat wasn't painting a romantic image for us that day in California, even if that's where my mind had gone. Rather, she was asking us to reconnect back in our ancestry to a time before our ancestors had been forced off their land or forced to work on other land, a time before they had seen the land as something to exploit or extract from, a time when they understood what it meant to live in community, and when the land was the most important member of that community. In some ways, she was asking us to reach back to a time before racial capitalism had robbed us of those foundational relationships. She was inviting us to bring that ancestral wisdom, which all of us have, however buried or otherwise forgotten, to our relationship with our community and the land today.

In 2021, I got to go on a weeklong retreat to a little town called Inverness near Bodega Bay in northern California.[86] A number of current residents were powerhouse community organizers in the earlier phases of their lives, and they got together and decided to occasionally spend a week with their adult kids nearby so that organizers of color in Oakland could get an immersion into the peace and nature of where the retired organizers get to live now.

When I arrived at the house where I was staying, I was given a gift by the organizers of the local Inverness program (done in partnership with the Windcall Institute). It was a beautiful piece of art with the following quote on it.

> If people stay long enough, the spirits will begin to speak to them. It's the power of the spirit coming up from the land. The spirits and the old power aren't lost, they just need people to be around long enough and the spirits will begin to influence them.
> —Crow Elder

It feels like Crow Elder is offering the same wisdom, in a different fashion, as Pat.

Land acknowledgments have increasingly come into fashion in some social justice circles as a way to reconnect with the land and honor its Indigenous inhabitants. Some people have just learned about land

---

[86]If you happen to be a community organizer or nonprofit leader, you should look up the Windcall Institute, whose mission is to reduce burnout among movement leaders (particularly although not exclusively people of color), including fully funded retreats like the one I got to attend.

acknowledgments and its practice immediately causes something in them to shift. For others, it has become performative already. Land acknowledgments are a chance for a community to acknowledge publicly, such as at an event or at a board meeting or during worship, the original inhabitants of the land on which they gather, and sometimes to name how they are working or will work with Indigenous people today to heal their relationship with the land or return the land to Indigenous control.

The practice of a land acknowledgment is a response to what is sometimes called "settler colonialism." In an article about engaging in land acknowledgments in constructive ways, the essay defines the term:

> Settler colonialism is a persistent social and political formation in which newcomers/colonizers/settlers come to a place, claim it as their own, and do whatever it takes to disappear the Indigenous peoples that are there.[87]

The article goes on to quote Corrina Gould, who engages in the work of land rematriation[88] for the Ohlone confederated tribe, a nation without federal recognition on the land also called Oakland and Berkeley and San Francisco and San Jose. In a presentation she gave, Corrina said the following:

> Today we go across to many different territories whenever we get in our car or on a plane or on a bus, and never acknowledge the thousands of ancestors that were there and whose territory we're on because we have no relationship. Land acknowledgment must begin with a relationship with the people on whose land you are on. We can say words. Many universities right now, [in the] UC System and other places are looking for the words. "Give me the words that I can say at the beginning of each meeting, at the beginning of each graduation." Corporations "tell us the words we're supposed to say to acknowledge your ancestors." But are those corporations or universities or community centers doing work with the original people of the lands? And that's where it comes for me, the deep meaning, to acknowledge that you're on someone else's homeland.

---

[87] https://abeautifulresistance.org/site/2020/1/19/land-acknowledgments-in-neopagan-ritualsnbspperspectives-from-ohlone-territory

[88] I just love the term "rematriation," which kind of comes from a place of "well, the men didn't always do great with the land when they were in charge of it; this time when it gets returned, maybe we give it to the women instead."

When I talk to fourth graders, I say, "When you go to your best friend's house, how do you behave yourself?" And they'll say, "Well, we say thank you and please. We don't break people's stuff. We ask. We don't rummage through the refrigerator." Right? Those are things that, as adults, we teach our children and grandchildren. But as adults, do we do the same thing when we come to someone's territory? Because you're in someone else's home. Do we continue to say, "Thank you and please?" Do we not break things? Do we take care of things like they're our own or better?

And so, land acknowledgment comes with all those things as well. So, I think we've grown in leaps and bounds over the last twenty years, when nobody knew us at all, that people are coming to us, looking to us for guidance about what those words could be. I think the next step I'm looking for is how do we now live in reciprocity with one another on our homelands? No one is going home. This is becoming other folks' home as well. We want to be good hosts. And we need good guests. So, when I look at land acknowledgment today, I want to say, "Yes, I want to create those words." I want us to remember the genocide that happened on these lands. I want us to remember how people are now coming to our lands looking for a home. I want us to remember that we, as human beings, need to see each other as human beings again.[89]

Here, I think Corrina, like Pat, is saying there is a place to which we are all indigenous. There is a place where we all are hosts. Some of us have been forced away from that place. Others of us, through conquest, have lost our connection to that place. In instances where we've had to relocate, we're allowed to engage the people indigenous to that land to see if we may stay there even though the land isn't ours. We just never do that.

Which, now that I think about it, is pretty weird. I mean, what would happen if we could say, "Hey. I'm on this land because my ancestors lost their way. I'm trying to figure out how to be on it in a different way. There's no longer a place that I can identify as my people's land. What is the way I can be on this land in ways that honor and support you?"

---

[89]https://abeautifulresistance.org/site/2020/1/19/land-acknowledgments-in-neopagan-ritualsnbspperspectives-from-ohlone-territory. NOTE: to learn more about Corrina's phenomenal work, visit https://sogoreate-landtrust.org/

While I have watched the ritual of land acknowledgments encourage people to go deeper in their understanding of their relationship to the land and to the Indigenous land rights movement, here are some interesting reflections from Indigenous artists who have been witness to them in practice for a long time.

> If I'm going to see a show, I would prefer that the artist says something about how they feel about the practice of Land Acknowledgments, and then acknowledge the land we're on. Contextualize things. For me, it's critical to acknowledge not only the land we're performing on but also my ancestors. My Mi'kmaq ancestors in Nova Scotia were told to forget their identity. What does this mean for us to be talking about the original caretakers of the land? If you were able to tell them about the future, I don't think they could imagine that any attempts at reconciliation would ever happen.
>
> —Syreeta Hector[90]

> We looked at the four nations most commonly recognized in Toronto Land Acknowledgments and then went to four communities where those people actually live. We chatted to the people there about the practice and there was a huge disconnect for them. A lot of people in the communities said they didn't like Land Acknowledgments. It felt like a eulogy. We were there, now we're not, and now it's yours. That sentiment came up a lot. But these people are alive. They are artists. And maybe the next step for arts institutions in acknowledging these people is actually hiring them for their art.
>
> —Falen Johnson[91]

> It feels like many institutions are checking their box. It's on their to-do list, which negates the point completely. Name the nations, but also say what your relationship is to the land you're on. What's the history? It really bothers me when it's recorded, when it feels like it was a task, when it's impersonal, when it's looped in with announcements.
>
> —Yolanda Bonnell[92]

---

[90]"Indigenous Artists Tell Us What They Think About Land Acknowledgments," Graham Isador, Vice.com, August 9, 2019. https://www.vice.com/en/article/j5yxbd/indigenous-artists-tell-us-what-they-think-about-land-acknowledgments
[91]IBID.
[92]IBID.

All of these frustrations and critiques, as well as the few affirmations of the practice, tie back to (a) contemporary Indigenous people being seen and named and (b) participants in the land acknowledgment being moved to tangible action. As with any ritual, it takes refining and adapting.

We sometimes think of rituals as solidly locked into one pattern. But who was the first person to say, "why only a bar mitzvah? What about a bat mitzvah?" Rituals evolve in response to community needs and desires and learnings, while preserving the essential core (for a bar/bat/b-mitzvah, the core being introducing a youth to the congregation through the lens of their new responsibilities and their commitment to living a good and faithful life at the age of discernment). The same can be true of a land acknowledgment, whose core is the recognition of what was, what harm has occurred, and what repair can be done (in solidarity with and with guidance from Indigenous people today). Talk about a connection to the Emerging Stories of the Storytelling Project Model.

Along those lines, I was recently co-teaching a class with my friend Deb, in which she began the session with a land acknowledgment and then invited people to introduce themselves. My friend Regina was taking the class and at the beginning of her introduction she said, "I would like to also pause and make a labor acknowledgment. My ancestors' blood and sweat and tears soaks the land on which I live and soaks the land of this whole nation."

> My ancestors' blood and sweat and tears soaks the land on which I live and soaks the land of this whole nation.
> — Regina Evans

When Regina said that so powerfully (she is a playwright, so figures), I was reminded of a line from Colson Whitehead's novel *The Underground Railroad* that will never leave me. One of the main characters, an enslaved woman about to free herself, looks out on the land she's been forced to tend her entire life, and she thinks about the people driven from that land. "Stolen labor on stolen land" is her simple observation, a chilling summary of a huge part of our nation's history.

Some of us were or have ancestors who were driven from other lands by war or famine or political violence.

Some of us have ancestors who were forced here as prisoners or were enslaved.

Some of us were or have ancestors who were forced here by economic destabilization abroad.

Some of us can trace our ancestors on this land back thousands of years.

Some of us did come here for a better life. Some found it.

Now, as we live on this land together, we are invited by friends alive and ancestors from before to remember a time when the land didn't belong to us but we belonged to the land. Our accountability to our ancestors in this instance leads to accountability to the ancestors on this land, which leads to accountability to the land itself. And if we do that accountability well, wherever we do find ourselves will call us into relationship with and accountability to those who are the descendants of this land's ancestors.

Perhaps this particular form of connecting with ancestors will allow us to co-create repaired work on repaired land, healed work on healed land, and thriving work on thriving land.

Continuing The Work, Continuing The Relationship Building

WHERE WE CAN GO FROM HERE

○ *If you want to write and reflect on this chapter's theme in your own life:*

Write what it is you want to say to the ancestors on whose land you live. What questions do you have? What reflections do you want to offer? What commitments do you want to make?

○ *If you want to engage a personal ritual around this chapter's theme:*

It is always a good idea to learn the name of the people on whose land you live. As of the printing of this book, you can find that information at https://land.codeforanchorage.org/

Light a candle to honor those ancestors. Share with them a reflection on what you value about their land and how you want to be in deeper relationship with the land.

○ *If you want to engage your activist or spiritual group in a practice that will help them begin to connect with ancestors in new ways as part of their work to dismantle white supremacy:*

The Oakland Peace Center had a land acknowledgment at every staff meeting, event, and gathering. The OPC land acknowledgment had these elements:

- Remembering that the land we inhabit was stolen from people who stewarded it and did not consider it a commodity.

- A recognition that the people from whom the land was stolen are still alive and in our midst.

- A commitment on our part to be in deeper relationship with that Indigenous community and also to de-commodify land in tangible ways.

Explore engaging in a similar land acknowledgment for your group. And discuss what you know about the Indigenous people in your community (potentially including people in your own group).

Chapter Ten

Claiming Our Ancestors as Part of Our Journey to Wholeness

> *Some people are your relatives but others are your ancestors, and you choose the ones you want to have as ancestors. You create yourself out of those values.*
>
> —*Ralph Ellison*

My friend Julie shared with me her reflection on a film called *Hidalgo*. As she describes the movie, it's about how a white-passing Indigenous man must come to terms with who he is, and whose he is, in order to thrive. (It's also about horses.)

The journey we've been on together includes some of the same elements. It has involved some heavy lifting, but there's also a big payoff. When we tell the whole stories of our ancestors, all of our ancestors, we learn better who we are and whose we are, and we end up a little more free. We end up being able to be in better relationship with each other because we're not haunted by the things we weren't in touch with before.

As we wrap up this massive ancestral journey together, let's take a moment in this chapter simply to appreciate what things can open up for us individually and within our communities as a result of the work we have done. Let's also look, a little bit, on what we can do to continue integrating those ancestors, now that we know them a little better, for the sake of our work of justice.

Wilfred Buck is a co-curator at the Canada Science and Technology Museum. He runs a program called Tipis and Telescopes, where he teaches Indigenous teachers, students, and community leaders to read the constellations of the night sky the way his Cree ancestors did. (According to the journalist covering the story, he does this even when it means sleeping out in the very cold May evenings in Manitoba.)

At the museum, Buck, along with Dakota/Lakota and Ojibwe astronomer Anette Lee, tells the stories of the constellations for a wide-ranging audience. They do this work as part of the country's and the museum's commitment to restorative justice practices.

In addition to restorative justice, however, there is a critically important lesson about the nature of wisdom and knowledge and who has historically been allowed to claim them. "As much as there's this idea that science is all rational, science is immune from culture, that's simply not true. Science itself is not actually separate from culture," Lee says. "It came from a specific culture, and that's Western European."

Lee means that our very picture of science was shaped by Western European history and the biases of that culture.

But science is something anyone can do, and, Lee says, everyone has done. The process on paper is simple: closely observe the world, test what you learn, and transmit it to future generations. That Indigenous cultures have done so without test tubes doesn't make them unscientific, she says, just different.[93]

When my best friend from high school turned forty and organized an amazing adventure to celebrate, I had the very rare privilege of doing the four-day hike of the Inca Trail with an Indigenous guide (and a team of Indigenous people who carried our tents and cooked our food and ran the trail in flip-flops, arriving at each camping spot at least an hour before the first of us Americans and often three hours before I joined the crew). Because I lagged behind by so much, I ended up getting to spend a lot of time with the guide who couldn't leave me

---

[93]"Relearning The Star Stories Of Indigenous Peoples: How the lost constellations of Indigenous North Americans can connect culture, science, and inspire the next generation of scientists," Christie Taylor, Science Friday, September 6, 2019. https://www.sciencefriday.com/articles/indigenous-peoples-astronomy

on my own (for fear of being fired by the company if word got back down the mountains).

He spent a lot of time explaining to me the incredibly advanced science of his Mayan ancestors prior to the invasion of European colonizers in Peru. As we hiked as high as two miles above sea level, he pointed out ruins that used to be scientific laboratories. He shared with me that in his own adult life, he had suffered from an illness that doctors and x-rays and cat scans couldn't diagnose. So, he brought in the village shaman, who killed a guinea pig, used the guinea pig to scan his body, and the sickness left him. He could sense my skepticism and said, "I tried your western medicine but the reason I am alive and pain free is the wisdom of my ancestors."

I'm not sure he was wrong to call it "my" western medicine. Despite coming from two ancient civilizations (no matter what the English tell you about either one), I tend to rely on modern science, which, as Dr. Lee points out, is only one form of science—not automatically more scientific, just different. Part of white supremacy culture is that we *all* internalize these ideas about the validity of certain types of knowing. As a result, over time, many of us have lost the stories and the knowledge of our ancestors.

Another student participant in Tipis and Telescopes, Jordyn Hendricks of the Red River Nation, said that the program turned her towards science after a lifetime of seeing it as irrelevant to her community, after a lifetime of having her people's contributions devalued. "We're seen as primitive or not super smart. But we were super smart," Hendricks says. "And it's important to bring that in and recognize it."[94]

⟪⟪⟪⟪⟪⟩⟩⟩⟩⟩⟩

I grew up in the Midwest. When people heard my parents' accents and asked where they were from, my parents said, "Akron." They weren't being snarky; that is how they thought of themselves. (Well, maybe they were *also* being snarky. I love my parents.)

---

[94]"Relearning The Star Stories Of Indigenous Peoples: How the lost constellations of Indigenous North Americans can connect culture, science, and inspire the next generation of scientists," Christie Taylor, Science Friday, September 6, 2019. https://www.sciencefriday.com/articles/indigenous-peoples-astronomy

When I went to college on the East Coast, I made a friend who said that even though she was in school there, she was most definitely a west coast person. I hadn't known the world broke down into these categories. When I came home and told my parents, full of anticipation and excitement, that I thought I was an east coast person, my mother was nonchalant. "Well, yeah. There's a reason that every time we had a week off, we would go to the ocean. Your father grew up on water. I grew up on water."

It hadn't dawned on me that my parents weren't necessarily "Midwest people." They wanted to live in community with people who were kind and decent and hardworking like them, as Midwesterners are generally understood to be. But my parents had ancestors on the water. We were always going to be more at home on the water.

It wasn't that different from when I was in seminary. A friend and I teased our other friend Chris about how he managed to visit Cameroon when he was such a fussy eater here in the US. He shrugged casually. "As soon as I got there, I knew it was the food of my people."

When I was still the director of the Oakland Peace Center, I invited a colleague to do a workshop with us on the enneagram, one of the popular personality tests that helps people make sense of why they engage the world together the way they do, based on a circle with nine different types of human engagement with the world.

It was a little surprising, to me more than anyone, that I had extended this invitation. Back in the early 2000s. I had to complete an enneagram questionnaire during a three-day psychological evaluation process before I could be ordained. This is standard practice and is largely well-intentioned.

As part of this process, we had to answer questions about ourselves, but my embedded cultural training taught me never to be self-affirming. As a result, my test scores indicated I was a terrifying authoritarian in the making. (Fortunately, this was on day three, and the evaluators by then knew something was going on that gave me such skewed results.)

But one thing stuck out to me at the time. The evaluators explained the origin of the test as they understood it. It had been adapted by practitioners in the United States as a self-administered test, but originally it emerged from Bedouin tradition. In that practice, the community would gather in a circle and say to one another, "Here's this thing you do that harms the community. Work on that so we don't die out here in the desert."

I felt super vindicated. My test results may have said I was a bully, but I was just channeling a Bedouin survival circle. (Hey, it made me feel better at a very vulnerable time.)

I've never quite let go of that version of the enneagram story, even though the conventional wisdom these days is that you should never "type" someone else.

So, when my colleague, an Asian American pastor from Silicon Valley, came and walked the OPC team through the enneagram (which was really fun, by the way), I asked him if that Bedouin story was true, half afraid that I'd have to let go of it when he, trained in this modality, told me it wasn't. But his response was different than I expected. "I've never heard that," he said, "but it gives me goosebumps. That's usually ancestors telling me there's truth to listen to." (Asian wisdom for the win! Also, if you have data that this story is wrong, do not tell me. Please.)

All of these stories, I think, are just me acknowledging that for most of us, this feeling around for ancestors doesn't necessarily have much science to it. That can be frustrating, and it can sometimes lead us down the wrong path (I'm serious; don't tell me if the enneagram's not originally from the Bedouins). But sometimes, we simply encounter what I can only describe as magical connections, connections that jump back multiple generations—me and the ocean, Chris and Cameroonian food.

How do we keep those explorations and pathways open? How do we integrate our ancestors into our lives? In this chapter, we'll look briefly at how we can continue to integrate ancestors through spiritual practices, rituals, and stories, all of which we've talked about throughout the book already and are just consolidating here so we can think about them in practical terms.

Reconnecting with Spiritual Practices

My friend Tai Amri was my student minister and then my co-pastor at First Christian Church of Oakland. He helped midwife the Oakland Peace Center into existence before moving to a piece of land in Kansas where his family and friends are building collective community in relationship with the land and its ancestors.

Tai Amri was recently initiated into the Ifa tradition. "It's making me think," he wonders, "how might that be perceived on the continent? What are the questions around that initiation? My process is that I'm not initiating myself, but I'm being initiated by a priest who traces his lineage and was initiated in Nigeria. The most important altar in my house is my ancestral altar. I'm going to be initiated by a priest and receive my *ilekehs* (beads) from a priest, even though I know you can buy them on the internet."

What Tai Amri is pointing to, as are friends reconnecting with bruja and Voodon and pagan and other ancestral practices, is that there are good ways to engage ancestral practices, and there are bad ones. Again, many of us are feeling this out by touch and intuition, but I think ta few rules have emerged:

- Connecting with ancestral practices requires doing some research into your roots. What did people in the community of your ancestors do that helped ground the community?

- Connecting with ancestral practices does not require continuing elements that do harm or diminish others. Was your ancestral priesthood only available to men for example? Do the ancestors still need you to shut people out on those grounds?

- Connecting with ancestral practices requires community. You can learn things on your own, through books, online. But if you're engaging in ancestral practices, those practices were formed *in* community and were formed *by* community. Hence, Tai Amri's warning that buying ritual beads on the internet does not create authentic connection to the Ifa tradition.

- Connecting with ancestral practices does not necessarily require rejecting your current faith, although it may involve that, depending on how you're relating to your ancestors. Some of us connect with the divine through our current traditions, and learning that there are ancestral versions of those traditions which are liberative has been life-giving. For others, our current traditions have caused too much harm for us to find them redeemable. Some people have found ways to practice one tradition while also tapping into elements of their ancestral practices (some call this syncretism; others say this is just what religion always is). Some people practice their current tradition in ways that preclude tapping into other traditions (and while I think that's a huge loss, I know that for many years, I described myself as a Christian who appreciates Hinduism as opposed to someone with a stake in both traditions, for that exact reason).

- We can appreciate others' ancestral traditions, but it is generally harmful to adopt or appropriate them. A way of avoiding that is by practicing ancestral practices in community with people who have an unbroken lineage to that tradition.

- Even following these rules, it's possible to connect with spiritual practices that are harmful. I can think of Hindu communities with unbroken lineage to ancestral practices, and one of the practices they continue is casteism. Non-Hindus who are immersing themselves in what they find healing about those practices do not realize they're propping up casteism. In fact, many people with Hindu ancestry don't realize it either. So, for us, you and me, the ones engaged in this journey *for the sake of our contribution to justice*, we have to bring an additional lens when engaging our own and others' ancestral traditions and practices. Some people call this a hermeneutic of suspicion, where we engage practices with an eye to how they land with and on people directly impacted by societal inequities:

  - How does this ancestral practice connect us with the healing of ancestral relationships that caused harm?

  - How does this ancestral practice connect us with the healing of our relationship to the land?

  - How does this ancestral practice create opportunities for us to be in more just relationship with those around us?

Reconnecting with Ritual

There is a gift our ancestors have given us if we can dig deep enough to find it: ritual. For the purpose of this book, I'm distinguishing ritual from ancestral practice because the rituals may be ancestral, *or* they may simply be contemporary rituals that connect us to our ancestors. I know churches that engage in rituals around Samhain or Dia de los Muertos or the pouring out of libations depending on the makeup of the congregation. But even those rituals are often modernized practices designed to honor and celebrate the lives of ancestors we seek to honor and connect with, rather than fully adopting an ancient Celtic or Mayan ritual in the midst of worship or a board meeting or community event.

The need for ritual to guide us through hard seasons is powerfully summed up here in an article by Ari Honarvar.

> I don't know if I could have survived seven years of my childhood without the soul-saving rituals of my Persian culture. I grew up amid the Iran-Iraq War, which killed a million people. Besides the horrors of the war, freedom of thought and expression were severely restricted in Iran after the Islamic revolution. Women bore the brunt of this as, in a matter of months, we were forced to ditch our previous lifestyle and observe a strict Islamic attire, which covered our bodies and hair. We lost the right to jog, ride a bicycle, or sing in public. Life seemed unbearable at times, but we learned to bring meaning into uncertainty and chaos by maintaining grounding practices and developing new ones.[95]

There's a lot of science that explains the positive and healing effects of ritual—on our levels of anxiety, our general mood, and even on our confidence. There is research that shows chanting in Sanskrit does something to your limbic system. The science is out there. And it doesn't need to be ancient rituals for the health benefits. Brand-new, made-up ones will work, too!

What makes a ritual is repetition more than age. I mentioned in an earlier chapter that a healthy part of my mother's dealing with being disowned was creating new traditions. My father's favorite, even though he was Hindu, was the Advent teas we had on the four Sundays leading up to Christmas, with the lighting of candles on a wreath on the table and, more importantly, little finger sandwiches and sausage rolls and mince pies.

But on our journey with ancestors, there are solid reasons for delving into rituals that connect us with ancestors. We already discussed what it means to connect with spiritual ancestors, and part of that is most easily done through rituals. The structure of a Passover Seder can have very culturally relevant and contemporary elements, and it also connects its practitioners to the experiences of their ancestors in bondage. The fifty-

---

[95]https://www.yesmagazine.org/issue/good-money/opinion/2018/12/20/why-rituals-are-good-for-your-health

year old ritual of Kwanzaa offers opportunities to engage in practices and values that are counter to the dominant culture in ways that can bring African American families together around shared practices connecting them to histories this country has tried to take away.

In the same article, Honarvar shares how rituals helped her get through seasons of hunger. Families would gather and tell an old, old story about a little girl who had run away from an abusive family. Angel aunties came to her and told her to make sweet halwa and give it to the poor, to work for the ingredients or borrow them. Honarvar said that the families on rations also each brought an ingredient, so each person ended up with a taste of sweet halwa and a wish, as well as a sense of connection to each other and to a story that had carried many generations through hard times.

Practicing rituals that connect us to ancestors can have varying levels of difficulty. A significant factor in making that connection easier is finding things about those ancestors we can relate to, whether mundane or sacred, a daily practice or a behavior pattern.

The island my mother's people come from, Great Cumbrae, has three active churches for their village of about a thousand (plus thousands more when the day trippers come over from Glasgow on bank holidays and in the summer). When my mother and I visited in 2019, we went to Sunday service at the Scottish Presbyterian church for most of the month. Each week, using the prayers from their prayer book, they prayed for safety for people whose livelihood came from the sea.

One Sunday, my mother left the island and went on a tour "of all the places in Scotland Americans have been that I never visited when I lived here," she said, "so I have to stand there stupidly as they tell me about them and say, 'och aye that sounds lovely.'" I used the opportunity to visit the Cathedral of the Isles, a Scottish Episcopal church (the smallest cathedral in Britain) because my mother is allergic to high church and would never have gone with me. Crammed into the choir stalls, we read a prayer from the Book of Common Prayer I had never seen before, which prayed for sailors before singing "For Those in Peril on the Sea." I didn't have time to visit the Catholic church in town, but I would wager they do the same.

Each time they pray those prayers, the faithful Christians of Millport are remembering people today since their only connection to anyone beyond the edge of town requires taking the ferry. They are praying for people today as they watch members of the Royal Navy deploy somewhere and practically fly down the Firth of Clyde, as they did on the way to Iran during our visit.

And every time they offer that prayer, they are remembering those the island lost in World Wars I and II. They are remembering ancestors swept away in dangerous waters who lived on the sea and died on it.

Their lives today hold a thread that connects them back many generations.

The further removed we are from the experiences of our ancestors, the more intentional we have to be about engaging in curiosity and empathy as we create rituals that connect us to them. When we do engage in rituals that honor the experiences of our ancestors, they may bring a deeper connection and cause us to see the world and those around us differently.

I went to a spoken word event for, by, and of several organizations that work with youth of color a while back. The groups represented Black youth, Latine and Indigenous youth, and Asian and Pacific Islander youth, all of whom faced a great deal of disinvestment in our community.

One of the Black elders offered an opening ceremony with the ritual of the pouring of libations, which he had learned from spiritual mentors in Ghana.

> **The fruit of relationship and trust-building is that we can lend our ancestral rituals to the people we know will value and not misuse them.**

He told the youth gathered there that they were all connected by water and by ancestors, and he poured out libations in honor of those ancestors who had been lost to the water and those who had survived. He poured out libations to honor immigrant and refugee and enslaved ancestors. He poured out libations for the earth that sustains us all. He honored the tradition of his ancestors, and he shared it and included all of us in it.

In an era where we seek not to misappropriate each other's cultures, it was a beautiful reminder that the fruit of relationship and trust-building is that we can lend our ancestral rituals to the people we know will value and not misuse them.

There's one other way to think about ritual I'd like to add to the mix.

In 2021, I got to be part of a group discussion with some people trained around the issue of moral injury, including my mentor Rita Nakashima Brock. We read an article together called "Decolonizing moral injury studies and treatment approaches: An Africentric perspective."[96] The article argued for the role of ritual in healing trauma, illustrating it with how Indigenous rituals had been used to help child soldiers process moral injury and how a family with an abusive husband/father did the same.

During that conversation, I remember Rita talking about her colleague Peter Storey, who had worked on South Africa's Truth and Reconciliation Commission, saying, "The only thing the perpetrators got was amnesty." What a chilling reflection on the state of the ancestors many of us inherit: getting away with the harm they've done but left alone, ill-equipped to do the healing work they need to do. How much more powerful to engage ancestral rituals in the work of moral injury, restorative justice, and transformative justice to heal those in our midst. Perhaps we will even find that those rituals can also help us heal those ancestors.

That day, Rita also shared the story of a Native American code talker from World War II who could not put his life back together when he returned from war. As Rita told the story, he said that the ghosts of the Japanese soldiers wouldn't leave him alone. His family invited everyone willing to dedicate as much time as it took to ritually help the ghosts, and him, find peace. That meant the family had to be willing to feed everyone who came offering help for as long as it took, and everyone who came had to stay for as long as it took.

And they did. They hoped to heal the ghosts, that they might heal the survivor, too.

What's particularly important about that ancient ritual was that it required the investment of the whole community in the man's healing. For us to engage ritual in the work of healing and justice will require the whole community.

---

[96]https://journals.sagepub.com/doi/abs/10.1177/09593543211027228?journalCode=tapa

Reconnecting with Stories . . . All the Stories

While we were still on Great Cumbrae, my mother's second cousins came to the island to visit. We had a great time touring the museum on the island (where they found a picture of their father in one of the exhibits!), having a pub lunch, and having tea and chatting in the little flat I had rented.

As I shared a little of the work I was doing, they affirmed me, and my cousin said, "Oh, you remind me of the Tartan Pimpernel!" I hadn't heard of him, but my third cousin enthusiastically and proudly explained that Donald Caskie, the "Tartan Pimpernel," was a Church of Scotland pastor who, during World War II, helped rescue 2,000 German prisoners of war and aided their escape to freedom.

"Of course, then he went on a tour of churches telling the story and selling his books," my cousin said disappointedly, as if that undid all that good work. In Scotland, there are few sins worse than self-aggrandizement.

Two things struck me as true: (1) I've never done anything like the Tartan Pimpernel. (2) A story kept silent for modesty's sake would never have made its way to a church hall where my cousin would hear it and then be able to relate it to me as part of my cultural heritage. So maybe self-aggrandizement is not the worst sin after all.

There are surely other stories from my heritage I need to know and to tell.

My friend Ashe shared with me how some of her work with the Jesus Radicals, a group of Christian anarchists,[97] seeks to dismantle a toxic empire in ways akin to the task of Jesus and his disciples in the time of the Roman Empire. Our colleague, Ched Meyers, at one point in their work together asked the question, "How are you supposed to do the work of revolution if you don't know the history of the movement?"

---

[97]You may already know this, but I have run into enough people who aren't familiar with anarchism as a political philosophy that I feel I should mention: anarchism is the belief in the dismantling of governmental systems and in the establishment of co-operative, people-run systems in their place. I sometimes joke that it's like if libertarianism actually cared about people. It's premised on the understanding that most governmental systems actually serve white supremacy and an extraction economy, so if for any reason anarchism feels far-fetched, who was disproportionately harmed during the government's handling of the Covid crisis is a good case study for why people become anarchists.

Ashe shared how in the Catholic Worker movement, "there's an understanding that you have to know your saints and know your lineage." Then she asked the important question (acknowledging that she does so from a Protestant experience which has a dearth of practice with knowing the saints at all), "How do we do that from a confessional space? Older Catholic Workers want to venerate [people like Dorothy Day and Peter Maurin who founded the movement], whereas younger people in the movement will say, 'but here's how Daniel Berigan [of the movement] was an asshole also.' . . . Some of how we're screwed up is through these very people."

I have a photo I took at a conference or a worship service; I can't quite tell. It's of a screen bearing this quote:

> Where common memory is lacking, where people do not share in the same past, there can be no real community. Where community is to be formed, common memory must be created.
> —Georges Erasmus, Dene Nation, co-chair of the Royal Commission on Aboriginal Peoples (Canada)

The words of Erasmus get at the fullness that Ashe and others throughout this book point to. We are inheritors of a legacy that shapes us. If we don't know those stories, that legacy can misshape us or is misshapen itself. We have an obligation to tell stories if we want to understand ourselves, particularly if we want to understand ourselves in relation to each other. We cannot actually build what Dr. King called "Beloved Community" if one person acknowledges the ancestors that he lost during the Middle Passage and another denies her ancestors who worked on those ship decks, for example.

> To poison a nation, poison its stories. A demoralised nation tells demoralised stories to itself. Beware of the storytellers who are not fully conscious of the importance of their gifts, and who are irresponsible in the application of their art.
> —Ben Okri

I will contribute more fully to the labor movement if I know my history, that I had ancestors who immigrated here, helped build the Brooklyn Bridge, and then were part of the ex-migration because they would rather die poor with their own people than be exploited and die on land whose leaders hated them.[98]

I will show up more fully to the work to fight caste oppression knowing that my family benefited from that system for millennia and knowing what happened to the ancestors who were caste-oppressed.

I do my work in Oakland differently because I have learned the stories of the Black Panther Party, what they faced, how they rose up for justice, and how the government killed them and infiltrated and undermined their movement.

Learning about the Ohlone shellmounds, Indigenous ancestral places to honor the dead in my community, means that I am less likely to shop at the shopping plaza built on a shellmound (on a street called Ohlone Way) and more likely to join the annual Indigenous day of mourning on that site, a way of making sure the community knows the full stories of where they live and on whose land they shop.

My friend Barbara shared this quote a while back:

> The Aboriginals looked up at night and they didn't see the stars—they never saw stars. They only saw the campfires of their ancestors on their journey. The bright stars were the ancestors who were not long gone; the dimmer stars were the ancestors further on the journey. They imagined that the ancestors sitting around their campfires were looking back and seeing the campfires of the living, physical, Aboriginals at their own campsites. The Aboriginals looked up and really believed that their eyes could meet.
> —Eddie Kneebone, Aboriginal teacher and activist

I love that. It reminds me of the words of Wilfred Buck, as he points out various Cree constellations: "And that's called Pakone Kisik. The hole in the sky. And the hole in the sky is where we come from."[99] Our origin stories are amazing. How our ancestors made sense of the world around them is amazing. How they passed on stories in ways we would be able to access millennia later, amazing. Rituals that meet our need to be connected, amazing.

---

[98]Profound gratitude to my grandmother's cousin Glen Caldwell for introducing that piece of history to my family's memory bank.

[99] https://www.sciencefriday.com/articles/indigenous-peoples-astronomy/

Our ability to look up and believe our eyes can meet the eyes of our ancestors, or see where we originated from, or see the power of our ancestors in the moon during 추석 ... our ancestors gave us gifts because they were invested in how amazing *we* are.

Claiming all of the ancestors also means telling the stories of our amazing ancestors, and all of us have them, ancestors who survived and struggled and overcame. It also means telling the stories of the ancestors who caused harm (and almost all of us have ancestors who caused harm—though, in many instances, the ancestors who survived ended up causing harm due to their trauma). As my friend Julie said, "We need to claim *all* of them, even when it is difficult to do so. That is how we get to that wholeness. We don't have to love or agree or even appreciate them to claim 'Yep. This is my history. Our history. How do we make it better?'"

My friend Christine added, "We may also find that this creates new communities of solidarity when we discover who else is claiming these ancestors—chosen, biological, or landscape."

Here is the remarkable thing about telling the truth: the truth may allow our ancestors to free us. The truth may help us set some ancestors free. The truth may help us free ourselves. As my mentor, the Rev. Phil Lawson, said at the launch of the Oakland Peace Center, "The opposite of enslavement isn't freedom. The opposite of enslavement is community."

> "The opposite of enslavement isn't freedom. The opposite of enslavement is community."
> —**Rev. Phil Lawson**

In the process of telling the full stories of our ancestors, we can make connections with others. We may have ancestors who faced similar struggles at different times. We may have ancestors who went through the things that bring us into the justice work we engage today. We may even have ancestors who were on opposite sides of the same struggle. Remember, what brought together the descendants of Dred Scott and James Taney was someone telling that full story and inviting the rest of the family to process it together.

Concluding Thought About Reconciling

In his interview on Amanpour & Co., Henry Louis Gates shared the following reflection on reconciling our ancestors into our lives:

> I don't think that you could embrace a universal cultural identity without having a particular culture on which to stand. And that's the same principle that's at work in "Finding Your Roots." We're all admixed. We all have been sleeping with each other for a long, long time. We all are Africans. The only question is if you are a distant African or a recent African. Yet, despite how different we look, at the level of the genome, we are 99.9 percent the same. We all come from the proverbial common ancestors, the proverbial Adam and Eve. And that's a marvelous thing to contemplate.[100]

I don't believe Gates is saying our particularities don't matter. I think he's saying that we need to balance our uniqueness with our universality. He's also arguing that our universality traces back to common ancestors *in Africa*, a continent that some of our ancestors have worked very hard to distance themselves from. The work he invites all of us into is reflecting on our and our ancestors' relationships to those, even earlier, common ancestors. That invitation offers us some remarkable opportunities for self-reflection, growth, and interrogation of both our ancestors and our contemporary community.

The particularities of our ancestries also matter, of course. What we notice about ourselves, what we know about ourselves, will aid us in uncovering the particular truths of our ancestors' lives.

For example, I have deep interfaith and interracial commitments. Those come primarily from growing up with my interfaith, interracial parents and experiencing the ways in which their relationship was not always accepted in broader society. So, let me be clear that I'm not saying it was necessarily ancestors who led me to that work. However, *because* that matters to me, I was more prone to notice at the Millport Museum at the Garrison (on the island of Great Cumbrae) the part of the historic exhibit that talked about how by the 700s, Picts and Celts and Angles and Britons shared the island, eventually also sharing it with Vikings. I can't help but notice that and ponder how that small island could hold

---

[100]Henry Louis Gates, on Amanpour & Co., 01.16.2020

multiple communities and multiple religions, and what that meant for their common life insofar as they had one.

In addition, because of my inclination more to what's right than to what's strictly legal or civil, I couldn't help but notice this part of the same exhibit, from the piracy section of the history of the island: "The Clyde teemed with smugglers in the 1700s. Legal goods had high taxes, so locals benefited from the activities of smugglers." The fact that the exhibit creators acknowledged the well-being of their ancestors as maybe more important than the law brings me a little bit of mischievous delight.

Finally, because I'm a deeply spiritual person and am also read as a woman in a professional arena where it's not always easy to be a woman, I'm particularly interested in St. Maura, who tended the sick on Great Cumbrae, and St. Beya, who died as a recluse on neighboring Wee Cumbrae, around the year 900 CE. Both are said to have taught women to study scripture, which meant teaching women to read in the year 900 CE.

Because of who I am, I encounter ancestors' practices and rituals and stories differently than I would if I had different life experiences. Engaging my ancestors along with others who have different life experiences might awaken me to different gifts the ancestors have to offer.

The last thing I want to offer regarding how to integrate our ancestors into our day-to-day life is this: interest in ancestors has increased in popularity in recent years. Along with it, there are more and more jokes about what wusses we are compared to our ancestors. And so I really love this social media post, which I found attributed to @lemonsharks on Twitter, as the final word on integrating our ancestors' love and wisdom and compassion in particular:

> My ancestors, watching me dump an entire stick of cinnamon, two cloves, an allspice berry, and a generous grating of nutmeg into my tea, sweetened with white sugar and loaded with cream, while I sit in my clean warm house surrounded by books, twenty-five plus outfits for different occasions, and six pairs of shoes, in a building heated so well I have the windows open in mid-autumn:

Our daughter prospers. We are proud of her. She has never labored in a field but knows riches we could not have imagined.

May we bring joy to the hearts of our healed ancestors because of the work of our own hearts. And may our work make the hearts of our unhealed ancestors squirm (more than) a little bit.

Where We Can Go from Here

○ *If you want to write and reflect on this chapter's theme in your own life:*

Write about the rituals, spiritual practices, and diversity of stories you plan to bring into your life and your community's life to stay connected to ancestors.

○ *If you want to engage a personal ritual around this chapter's theme:*

Let your ancestors know how you're going to engage them differently from this point on. Use any ritual practice that helps you feel grounded—candles, an altar, a breathing exercise, humming, praying.

○ *If you want to engage your activist or spiritual group in a practice that will help them begin to connect with ancestors in new ways as part of their work to dismantle white supremacy:*

Share with each other how you're going to tell the stories of ancestors differently, having been on this journey together. Tell the group a story the way you used to tell it, and how you'll tell it differently now, to change the next generation's relationship to its ancestors.

Chapter Eleven

Being the Ancestors Our Descendants Need

We are citizens of a land that has yet to be brought into existence, but nonetheless exists in the recesses of our long historical memories and revolutionary imagination.
—The Red Nation Podcast

When my mother walked with me to the graveyard toward the top of the island of Great Cumbrae, I got to hear great stories along the way. One was about a plant with huge leaves that grew on the other side of the big ditch on that road. The family called it the "Me Vont" plant because when my mother was very little, as my grandmother's youngest cousin, Glen, would push my mother in her pram, she would point to these plants whose giant leaves she liked to use as an umbrella and cry out "me vont!" Glen would have to climb across the ditch to get the leaves for his little cousin, Baby Dracula.

I was struck with a great sense of sadness when she told me this story, and it was largely for this reason: that story dies with me. I don't have children to whom I will pass along these family memories.

I would normally chide myself for being unnecessarily maudlin, but then I watched that episode of *Game of Thrones* from season eight, the episode which was so dark for most of the episode that I couldn't tell what was going on. Before the battle, the most beloved characters gathered and talked, and at one point, a character says something about how when the memory of us dies, it is our second death. Our body dies, and then the memory of us dies. (Yes, the Pixar movie *Coco* makes the point incredibly well also. I like dragons. Sue me.)

When all is said and done, my commitment to this work of connecting with ancestors has everything to do with this chapter. We learn from our ancestors in order to be the ancestors our descendants need. For some of us—me, for example—our stories may not live on in biological descendants. Our legacy will be in the contributions we make to the movement, to helping people work together to create a better world, to building community.

In one of the white people's wisdom circles that contributed to this book, someone said, "This work of telling the stories of our ancestors feels like holding the tension between celebrating and being honest. And my kids have done better with it. Gen Z will talk about mental health and shame and culture of inclusion better because they are being raised by people who learned to do it better than the people who raised us."

In working on this final chapter, I asked my friends about the kind of legacy they'd like to leave behind. What kinds of ancestors would they like to be? My friend Sara, who is raising children, offered this in response:

> This is what I've been thinking a lot in breaking various cycles in raising my own kids. In addition to wondering what story we want told of *us*, I wonder: How do we pass down the stories and understandings of our ancestors we have learned in such a way that our descendants will hear them and be able to do their own work of interpreting, dismantling oppressive systems, and healing trauma? In other words, what might our ancestors offer our descendants that we might not be in a place or situation to access?

In some of the anti-racism training I offer with my colleague Dave, he does a session on the Doctrine of Discovery. If he gets the sense that some white people are feeling a little defensive, that they think he's being harsh to the well-intentioned white people in the story, he says something along these lines: "Listen, some of them absolutely were trying their best. And they caused irreparable harm that crossed multiple generations. If my kids don't say the same thing about me—'he may have tried his best but also he seriously screwed up'—then I failed to raise them right. We *want* each generation to see what we got wrong because we *want* them to do better."

In some ways, what Dave is asking is, do you want to be well thought of, or do you want to make the world better? The way you engage your ancestors will, he suggests, answer that question for you.

My friend Deb and I did a series of workshops on Faith-Rooted Economics together back in 2017 or so. She had participants engage in a powerful exercise in which she would ask people to add to a timeline a story of a time their family's economic condition got better or worse. I remember one workshop where someone wrote that their family's economic situation got better in the 1940s because they were part of the Bracero program, and someone else in the room said her father owned a family farm that had survived because he had hired workers through the Bracero program. I mentioned that I knew people who had been forced off their land because of Japanese internment, which had led to a greater demand for farm workers and, subsequently, the creation of the Bracero program.

As it turned out, that was what Deb wanted us to see. As participants wrote up things that had happened in their family's economic history, their [collective] families' histories often lined up with major issues in the country, issues of justice and injustice and repression in ways they had never considered or expected. A white participant shared how hard life had become for his grandparents during the Depression. A Black participant shared that her grandmother told her that the Great Depression had actually helped her family because, for the first time ever, they had access to government programs under FDR.

While Deb did that exercise to help us understand the economic history of this country that had shaped our migration, immigration, enslavement, and displacement narratives for hundreds of years, her real purpose was to help us build more economic justice in the here and now. She wanted us to read today's economic conditions through the lens of impact—what will make things better for those who are the hardest hit during economic downturns and least helped by government uplift programs?

In other words, Deb has us plumbing the depths of our economic history in order to build a different economic future for the generations to come. As the saying goes, "We have not inherited the earth from our forefathers. We are borrowing it from our descendants." We know that trauma carries across three generations, and so does healing. We also know that it takes twenty years of absolutely nothing going wrong for someone to get out of poverty, and we know that on average, it would take a Black family 228 years of work to catch up to the wealth of the average white family.[101]

"Let us be the ancestors our descendants will thank."

—Winona LaDuke

And so, while I do not have rigorous prescriptions for how to be better ancestors for our descendants (and while I'd be sad if you got to this point in the book and hadn't already begun to think of things that would allow you to make your own list), I will say that I think Winona LaDuke was thinking of these broad multigenerational injustices that are ours to reshape when she said, "Let us be the ancestors our descendants will thank."

The first third of this book was about the trouble with ancestors, including ancestral trauma. We talked about how trauma can be handed down epigenetically for several generations and the repercussions of our ancestors' actions can shape us for many more. (You know that saying "God give me the confidence of a mediocre white man?" That confidence comes from four hundred solid years of messaging.)

Here's some good news from the research I shared in the chapter on ancestral trauma.

> If trauma is shown to be passed down the generations in humans in the same way as it appears to be in mice, we shouldn't feel a sense of inevitability about this inheritance, says Dias.

> Using his cherry blossom experiments in mice, he tested what would happen if males that feared the scent were later desensitized to the smell. The mice were repeatedly exposed to the scent without receiving a foot shock.

---

[101]https://www.thenation.com/article/archive/the-average-black-family-would-need-228-years-to-build-the-wealth-of-a-white-family-today/

"The mouse hasn't forgotten, but a new association is being formed now this odor is no longer paired with the foot shock," says Dias.

It also suggests that if humans inherit trauma in similar ways, the effect on our DNA could be undone using techniques like cognitive behavioral therapy.

"There's a malleability to the system," says Dias. "The die is not cast. For the most part, we are not messed up as a human race, even though trauma abounds in our environment."

At least in some cases, Dias says, healing the effects of trauma in our lifetimes can put a stop to it echoing further down the generations.[102]

The American Psychological Association also shared some interventions around multi-generational trauma in relation to addiction. A program between researchers and a number of tribes, including the Ojibwe, Lakota, Dakota, Navajo, and Pueblo, the focus has been particularly successful as it reconnects families and community as a strategy for reducing early substance use. "We hear a lot about the loss of a sense of community, the loss of generational ties," says Melissa Walls, a sociologist from the University of Minnesota Medical School involved in the program. "It really is a deep hurt, a deep pain—almost a longing for what used to be."

"The results of these programs can be profound," says Walls, who describes a ceremony held at the end of each intervention. There, parents or caregivers give youngsters a blanket to symbolize their support of the next generation. "It's always powerful," she says. "It's a lot more than just a program, I think, for the people who get to do it."[103]

Another program some clinicians are using is the same as a pre-marital support project I learned in seminary, one of the first places I really began to look at my own ancestors and how they shaped me. The Director of Ministry taught us some basic tools for helping a couple who is getting married, and one was to invite each person to draw a relationship tree and then discuss how the family navigated the complexities of those

---

[102]https://www.bbc.com/future/article/20190326-what-is-epigenetics
[103]https://www.apa.org/monitor/2019/02/legacy-trauma

relationships and how it shaped them and their understandings of relationship. In a similar vein, several intervention programs are helping patients construct family trees that include family trauma, sometimes also incorporating pictures and family sayings that reinforced trauma. The advantage of this is transcending secrecy and deepening connection.

When dealing with news of present-day racialized horrors that connect back to original traumas (police shootings that connect back to a long history of racialized violence, for example), Breland-Noble works with her African American clients to name that connection to history rather than deny, downplay or ignore it, according to the American Psychological Association. "We're so used to living with racially oriented worry and fear that we don't necessarily recognize or name it as problematic," she says. "I want people to feel comfortable owning and naming our history." Even in working with children, a strategy that explains the context of that ancestral trauma, combined with cultural pride and coping strategies for when they encounter racism are helpful tools for healing.[104]

As we look at how to be better ancestors to the next generation, a lot of that is going to look like developing our own tools to deal with the ramifications of ancestral trauma that is regularly brought up again and against since the past lives on in the present, in our pain and our trauma and our unearned privilege, all of it. Being better ancestors will also be about having fuller, more helpful conversations with our children that equip them to understand their past and be prepared for their future, with a strong dose of stories of ancestors that make them feel supported and less alone in their work.

My friend Ashe has tried for huge swaths of her life to build community that would help white people process and heal from the harms of whiteness, and most of her experiences have left her feeling that white people are, at best, willing to look at it in terms of their own healing and their own efforts to make things right. The irony is not lost on her that loss of community orientation is one of the costs of whiteness over many generations in the first place. "I have a sense that why certain movements like Matewan worked is that community was built around what they were fighting for. But when it's about how to deal with internalized whiteness, that's really hard."

---

[104]https://www.apa.org/monitor/2019/02/legacy-trauma

A while back, Ashe reflected on what it means that we haven't been mentored by elders who wanted us to know these stories and see the models that were available to us. "I've spent my whole life without mentorship or eldership, and I'm screwed up," noted Ashe. "And I have to figure out how to support these younger white people who come to me looking for what I didn't get." Since that conversation, I've been reminded multiple times about how few elders and mentors those of us doing social justice work really have. We certainly have a handful of romanticized stories of mythic figures, but very few of us get a lot of wisdom and encouragement on how to do things differently.

In fact, about a year after my conversation with Ashe, I was on my podcast with some friends (if you like the famous cartoon about four little kids saving the world with the power of the elements at their side, you'll want to catch the podcast *Bending the Arc: Avatar the Last Airbender for the Global Majority*). We talked about the first episode, in which the village is largely devoid of men because of war. I mentioned that years ago, some of my female friends were talking about how hard it was to find emotionally available men our age in Oakland, and one of them said, "The thing we don't always think about is our men have been through a war." She was referring to the crack epidemic and the violence it wrought, both of which did so much harm to so many youths in that era. My roommate, who is male, said this was something women didn't understand: what it had been for men to live through that.

On the episode, another friend said, "Yeah, but also, Sandhya and I have talked a *lot* over the years about the lack of mentorship we had coming up. Women of color also grew up with trauma and without mentors in that era." It was a reminder to all of us that the traumas of our elders didn't get named to us and we didn't always have the tools to name them well to the next generation.

As we think about being better ancestors to our descendants, part of that work is picking back up the ancestral practice of intentionally shaping and mentoring the next generation, though with a big dose of humility. "We're learning how to do this. We may be doing this wrong, but we will show up for you." Because my experience over and over has been that young activists want the support of elders in the movement. They don't want preaching and lectures, necessarily, but they want to know that we believe in them and that we see ourselves in their work, which is what creates the opportunity for us to share. They are also hungry for the resources that come through knowing your ancestors.

I've been a part of a South Asian American youth activist camp a number of times during the past decade called Bay Area Solidarity Summer (BASS). In fact, that experience may have contributed to my sense of this book's importance for two reasons. First, hands down, the most impactful exercise for most of those youth is when Barnali and Anirvan lead them through the timeline of South Asians in the US, with a particular focus on South Asian American justice work and cross-racial solidarity. We don't ignore casteism or sexism or anti-Blackness or Islamophobia during the camp; in fact, a lot of our work focuses on that. But for South Asian American youth who didn't necessarily realize we have a long history in South Asia and also in the US of resisting injustice, it is an absolute balm; it makes them feel less alone in the world.

The other way BASS influenced this book is that the last summer I was on the core team (now I just occasionally do a workshop, meet a few youth so they can connect with movement elders, or cook a meal during camp), the folks who had been leading the initiative for a decade noted that each year, more of the young people asked if they could call us their language-specific equivalent of Aunty or Uncle. While some of us felt that we were a little too close in age for that to be accurate (I'm not; I'm totally old enough to be the mashi for a twenty-four-year-old), we knew what it meant. It meant they were looking for people who could support them as they made sense of their calling, especially when they were in family systems that would not support that calling or be able to offer them guidance.

Being the ancestors our descendants need will mean developing the practice of supporting the next generation of justice seekers—being imperfect elders who pass on what we've learned and trust that they will navigate it their own way and learn in the process—and to explain *why* we hope they'll continue to connect with the ancestors themselves as we show them how we're doing it.

"The most successful people in our society, the things they do for society are bad, so we have to reconfigure success," notes Ashe, which is part of our work. But she also notes how powerful the culture of white supremacy is—so that when white people do that work, it is seen as an act of rebellion. And maybe it is. "Whenever a white person is asked to see this history differently, it is threatening. Some of us have to do this work because there's no other way for us to stop being oppressive. It involves admitting we're miserable. Pulling at the corner of the wallpaper until people acknowledge they have a deeper longing."

For white people seeking to be better ancestors to the next generation, some of this work requires staying with and working through the resistance, as well as navigating the complex arithmetic of how gentle to be, how confrontational, how compassionate and how unyielding. "My family knows I don't think they're evil [for believing differently than Ashe about the politics and religion of justice]," Ashe illustrates. "But they know the democrats think they're evil. If I can create space, they might engage . . . so my nieces will ask what anarchism is, for example." But it has to stay at the human, relational level for that shift, that curiosity, to happen. "I've been a part of groups of white people trying to go deep. My attempts at intentional community didn't work because people come with heroics. Every intentional community everywhere has grandiose ideas." In other words, to be the ancestors our descendants need will require investment in relationship, work on a movement that is grounded in the practical even when it is casting a huge and powerful and necessary vision, and patience with people not yet being where we are *even while we do not tolerate harm to people on the margins*. That is a delicate balance. No wonder so many of us didn't get the mentors we longed for. And yet, at their best, that's exactly the mentoring our most healed ancestors offer.

The reality is that for people of color, so much of how success is defined in our society was shaped by white supremacy culture. As a result, if we're being honest, a lot of our work within our own communities won't be completely different from the work of our white family. We will have hard conversations with family who disagree and struggle and feel frustration with the movement. We will navigate how to create space so the next generation can engage us with curiosity even if their parents can't. I think of my friend Patricia, and how actively she's stayed in relationship with a sister whose politics are the opposite of hers because that's what family is, but also so she can talk about things like gender roles and sexual orientation and Indigenous spirituality with her nieces, so they will have a different access point to the world.

I think of how my family in India love me so much and do not buy most of my political beliefs, *especially* my beliefs about India and even more particularly about the marginalized experience of Muslims in India. We argued a lot during my last trip, which happened after the first time ever that our state of West Bengal had voted in Hindu Nationalist (BJP) leadership. Part of my argument was that our fathers often talked of a time when Hindus and Muslims lived together in their village in harmony and that the growing hostilities were not the only way it could be.

At the end of my visit, half of my family went on a trip to Kolkata with me for the last few days before I flew west. I took them on a walking tour of Kolkata one day, and the tour guide took us to the monument to the Black Hole of Calcutta, where a number of colonial military had died during a rebellion in 1756. In 1901, the Viceroy put up a controversial memorial, which Hindu and Muslim independence leaders came together to resist. One of my nieces cocked her head to the side and said loudly, "Did you say that Hindus and Muslims worked together on this?" The guide said that was correct. My niece gave me a meaningful nod. She's listening to history differently, and I think it will shape her work in the world in meaningful ways.

I believe that for many of us, white supremacy culture has disrupted our connection with our ancestors. Now sometimes, a first-generation immigrant of color will use their own life as a counterexample to this claim, and I usually say, "How invested are your kids in those rituals?" But sometimes, and this is certainly true for some South Asian first-generation immigrants to the US, that is the generation where the ancestral connections get cut for a number of reasons that require their own book. Please, dear God, don't make me have to write that book.

The long and the short of it is that there are exceptions to every rule; in different communities the challenges of maintaining ancestral connections arise in a myriad of ways.

It is our job, especially those of us seeking to create a better world through the work of justice, to reconnect to those ancestors. That, in and of itself, is part of the gift we give to our descendants.

Obviously, we will bring different insights to those ancestors' stories because of the landscape in which we live today. I love the story of my great-grandmother whose deep love for her son caused her to cry herself blind. But I'll also tell that story as a story of how patriarchy poisons us all, because her access to a livelihood shouldn't have hinged on whether she had male children. My interpretation of that powerful ancestral story is shaped by what my own elders have taught me (including two parents who raised me to be an independent feminist who cared about the thriving of people mistreated in society).

Hopefully, if we keep doing the work of our own healing, and perhaps the healing of ancestors, we will show up as better ancestors ourselves, and perhaps our descendants will help us continue to heal once we have left this life. Equipping our children to recognize how ancestral trauma came to be so they can respond to it better will be a radical, culture-shifting act that will, in turn, allow our children to be the ancestors their descendants need.

As we name how white supremacy culture shaped and misshaped our ancestors, as we reject the ways it has shaped and misshaped us, and as we seek a different way of living together,[105] we will become the Emerging Story in the Storytelling Project Model that allows our descendants to build out their own action and transformation.

---

[105]For an excellent list of antidotes to white supremacy culture, check out https://dei.extension.org/extension-resource/white-supremacy-culture/

Where We Can Go from Here

○ *If you want to write and reflect on this chapter's theme in your own life:*

Write about what kind of ancestor you hope to be, and which ancestors have prepared you for that.

○ *If you want to engage a personal ritual around this chapter's theme:*

Pull together images or objects to connect you with the diversity of ancestors:

- To the ones who did harm, name it and tell them how you are changing things.

- To the ones who were harmed, name it and tell them how you're creating a different world.

- To the changemakers, tell them they are not alone. Share with them what you know of change work in your community.

○ *If you want to engage your activist or spiritual group in a practice that will help them begin to connect with ancestors in new ways as part of their work to dismantle white supremacy:*

Share with each other one way you're going to seek to be the ancestors your descendents need, based on what you've learned from this book about who and what ancestors can be and offer.

Postscript

I love myself, I love my skin, and I love my history. I'm grateful for who I am, grateful for the people who made me, my ancestors, and I wouldn't change a thing.

—*Wunmi Mosaku*

I can't stop thinking about one of the people of color wisdom circles early on in 2021 that shaped this book. I really didn't know what I was doing. I'd had this theme in my head since late 2018 but even I wasn't quite sure what I was going to do with it.

But in the second POC circle, we talked about the power of names. That's when Chris shared a story of his family who were so wild and also so unified that even the racist sheriff in their town wouldn't cross them. It was when Vanessa talked about how missionaries had taken away Pilipino names and replaced them with Spanish names. We talked about colonizers' names and enslavers' names. We talked about being given names but not being given the full stories of the people for whom we were named. My friend Xochitl shared a powerful essay she had written on standing in the power of who we are and whose we are. Here is just one paragraph of it.

> I am Xochitl Alvizo, grand-daughter of Consuelo Mora—dark, strong and beautiful—from whom I witnessed female strength and nonconformity. I am Xochitl, daughter of Olga, teenage mom, survivor of patriarchy, a woman who to this day keeps charting her own way. I come from a long line of women, known and unknown, stretching back to Africa.[106]

In that moment, I realized that even though I didn't know what I was doing, I had a community of friends and colleagues and mentors, and

---

[106]https://feminismandreligion.com/2018/04/01/the-power-of-black-panther-by-xochitl-alvizo/

ancestors, who were invested in helping me make this meaningful for you, for me, and for the movement.

That matters to me because as I told you in the beginning, and as you probably know by now, the reason I wrote this book was (a) to strengthen and encourage my movement family, so they feel supported in their lifelong work of justice and healing and (b) hopefully also to motivate my spiritual family that they might feel emboldened to deepen their lifelong work of justice and healing. The people with the power are always five steps ahead of the people without, and the people with a little power have to get *really* organized and *stay* organized. We need all the tools we can get.

I was bemoaning how scattered the themes of my books are to a colleague. The first was on the history of people of color in my denomination. The second was a plea for cross-racial solidarity in the face of white supremacy, disguised as stories on race and religion. The third was covertly a community organizing handbook. The fourth was a progressive daily devotional. This one is about ancestors.

The friend I was complaining to said actually my books form an arc, and my publisher should really consider selling them as a bundle. She explained, "You made visible those who had been erased. Then you introduced us to each other across racial diversity. Then you gave us the tools to do justice. Then you gave us spiritual nourishment when we were fatigued in the work, particularly people of color. And now you're giving us a resource for sustainability so we can do the work for a lifetime and even across generations."

That made me feel better because while this book felt important to me, it also felt squishy. I worried people would read it for personal betterment and not see how it was about organizing. But maybe they will. Maybe you did. Or maybe you picked it up because you've been on the same journey as me, and you already are an organizer or a doer of justice in some fashion. This will help sustain us as we continue the work.

One beloved friend suggested I sit with the scripture from Acts 26:6 where St. Paul is on trial and says, "And now I stand here on trial on account of my hope in the promise made by God to our ancestors."

He suggested the phrase "Hope in the Promise Made by God to Our Ancestors" as a starting place for the title of the book. I immediately saw it as an inscription plate at the beginning of the book, and then it ended up here in the post-script. Partly I'm intrigued by it because Paul is literally arguing for his life in front of his own community, a community that sees him now as a threat. Some of the work we do around ancestry can cause rifts between us and our own people who don't want our whole story to be out there and available.

The debates about how we teach US history, whose statues stay up and whose come down, they all point to this same challenge. Ancestors are not simple. They are clearly very powerful. I think they can keep us company in this hard work and point us to our people as we do the work.

As I wrap up this book, I find myself wondering what Emerging Stories we are a part of in the Storytelling Project Model. And I wonder what emerging stories we are learning from each other that will lead us into transformation. I am so grateful for that model as a way of leading us through our collective journey with ancestors in a way that always pointed us back to community and justice. I can't wait to see what we build together with our ancestors supporting us from behind and our descendants pulling us forward. I am grateful to be an ancestor-in-training along with you.

Glossary

racism—I am grateful that many years ago I was trained in my anti-racism work by Crossroads Anti-Racism Ministry. They use a definition originally developed by Patricia Bidol-Padva in 1970, which is now in the Merriam-Webster dictionary:

Racism = Race Prejudice + Institutional/Systemic Power

While people often use *race prejudice* and *racism* as if they are synonyms, that ignores the distinct ways that race was shaped in the US. (I talk about this more in my book *Pre-Post-Racial America*.) There's a real danger of ignoring the way institutional and systemic power function to reinforce race prejudice in ways that preserve power for white people at the expense of people of color. The danger is that we will continue to focus almost exclusively on internal and interpersonal issues when (as I hear often from my colleagues at the organization Race Forward) the vast majority of how racism stays in place is because of institutions and structures.

white privilege—I trust that if you picked up this book, you're probably already aware that white privilege isn't about good people and bad people. It's about people racism was set up to harm (people of color) and people racism was set up to serve (white people). Most of the white people I work with don't want to have more access to resources or function in a power structure that favors them. Fortunately, they're willing to acknowledge that it exists even if they don't want it to, and the solution isn't just to opt out (spoiler alert: you can't). The solution is to work together to dismantle those systems, institution by institution.[107]

---

[107]If you're trying to help a friend understand how white privilege doesn't mean their life was easy, it just means race wasn't what made it harder, there's a now classic essay called "Explaining white privilege to a broke white person" that, if your friend can handle a few curse words, is an excellent starting place. https://ydekc.org/wp-content/uploads/2018/08/E_Sadberry_Explaining-White-Privilege-to-a-Broke-White-Person.pdf

white supremacy—I love the fact that so many of my white colleagues are stepping up and taking seriously that their role in addressing race and racism is to reflect on what whiteness means rather than just focusing on how to help people of color. By studying the impacts of how whiteness was created as a racial identity beginning several hundred years ago and evolving due to social considerations of the people on top, my white colleagues have embarked on some of the same work that this book is about: ancestors. Without the construction of whiteness, they would have different relationships with their ancestors, and so would people of color!

Influential activist and scholar Tema Okun has been working on addressing the culture of white supremacy since 1990. I'd like to share her definition from her website here.

> White supremacy culture is the widespread ideology baked into the beliefs, values, norms, and standards of our groups (many if not most of them), our communities, our towns, our states, our nation, teaching us both overtly and covertly that whiteness holds value, whiteness is value. It teaches us that Blackness is not only valueless but also dangerous and threatening. It teaches us that Indigenous people and communities no longer exist, or if they do, they are to be exoticized and romanticized or culturally appropriated as we continue to violate treaties, land rights, and humanity. It teaches us that people south of the border are "illegal." It teaches us that Arabs are Muslim, and that Muslim is "terrorist." It teaches us that people of Chinese and Japanese descent are both indistinguishable and threatening as the reason for Covid. It pits other races and racial groups against each other while always defining them as inferior to the white group.[108]

While the odds are that if you're reading this book, you've been fighting against this culture for a while now, I think it's important to acknowledge that whether we embrace, are unconscious of, or actively resist white supremacy culture, that it is very much the unspoken culture of this country—not only of extremists but of the country as a whole. Acknowledging that culture is part of what equips us to recognize and dismantle it.

---

[108]https://www.whitesupremacyculture.info/what-is-it.html

patriarchy—If sexism is the way in which institutions preserve power for men at the expense of women and people who don't fit into the male category of the (inaccurate) gender binary, patriarchy is sexism's partner in crime, like white supremacy is to racism. Patriarchy is summarized by Costa Rican journalist Alda Facio as "a present day unjust social system that subordinates, discriminates or is oppressive to women."[109]

intersectionality—Functioning in the background of this book is *intersectionality*. It is in all of our ancestors' stories. You might hear it in some social justice work, or you may even want to introduce it into that work.

Dr. Kimberle Crenshaw created this word in 1990 to capture the ways different forms of oppression intersect with each other. The story originated with Black women seeking employment in the 1970s at a car manufacturing plant in Detroit. Black men had fought for and won access to factory floor jobs through the US Freedom Movement (sometimes called the Civil Rights movement). White women had fought for and won access to administrative jobs due to the (white) feminist movement. Black women faced barriers to factory floor jobs because they were women and administrative jobs because they were Black. Their case went all the way to the Supreme Court, who shrugged their shoulders and said, "We got rights for Black men and white women. That's as much as we can do." The women in the case said they were "doubly oppressed," and the term *intersectionality* captures the ways systems of inequality intersect to create varied forms of oppression.

Sometimes people use the term to mean multiple identities, but it doesn't mean that. Our experiences of multiple oppressions and, in some arenas, our relative or absolute privilege will show up as we delve into stories of ancestors. A poor, white, immigrant woman in our ancestry dealt with classism and patriarchy and one generation of anti-immigrant sentiment. Her son might only deal with classism and benefit from patriarchy and whiteness. I myself face challenges as an immigrant but have the benefit of English being my first language and having an easy path to citizenship. My gender and age and sexual orientation and skin color and having parents with college educations all intersect in ways

---

[109]Facio, Alda, "What is Patriarchy?" 2013, translated from the Spanish by Michael Solis. This five page article is well worth a read if the term patriarchy is a new one to you, but you're not a fan of sexism. http://www.learnwhr.org/wp-content/uploads/D-Facio-What-is-Patriarchy.pdf

that give me relative privilege or oppression. And my ancestors navigated different intersections that matter, too.

The easiest explanation I heard from a colleague for intersectionality was this: "Intersectionality is all the rocks that get hung around my neck." She said that as a Black lesbian pastor with mental health challenges. To me, the thing about intersectionality is the same thing about the rocks: we don't often notice the rocks we *don't* have hanging around our necks. That's why I wanted to explain the term, even if I don't use it too much throughout the text.

Acknowledgments

This book is dedicated to my parents, my cousins in India, and my grandmother's cousin Glen in Canada, all of whom made sure I knew my ancestors.

To my Patreon supporters who made sure I had health insurance during 2021 when I started my anti-oppression consulting practice and sought to complete this manuscript.

To the Louisville Institute, which saw this project as not only valuable to my community of organizers and activists but as valuable to the church, and who invested in me receiving not only financial support so I could have time to work on the book but a week of orientation during a point in the pandemic when I was overwhelmed, isolated and depressed. I will never forget the small group leader and also my peers saying, "Rest is actually a valuable way to prepare for this work. Scheduling in rest and adjusting your timeline might even honor your work and your ancestors."

To everyone who commented on the proposal. People named what would help them in their work, what questions they had, where I could go further and deeper, where I could make richer connections. This book is better because you were willing to read the proposal before I sent it to Chalice Press.

To Chalice Press, for saying it was okay for me to share their proposal process with dozens of people so I could get that input and write a better book.

To the people who participated in the three year-long monthly wisdom circles that heavily influenced this book. The white people's wisdom circle, the people of color's wisdom circle, and the writers' wisdom circle each offered such different content (and forced me to start articulating questions and theories I had not yet done, because up until those circles, my theories mostly just lived in my head, which isn't the best place for an extrovert's thoughts to live). I legit miss y'all. Those circles really did give me life.

To Polly, Patricia, and Janet, for being amazing colleagues and friends and for extending incredible generosity in giving me spaces to write. I've never written a book where I had dedicated time and space for the project. It spoiled me, and I'm not complaining.

To Nash, who typed up my sticky notes from the Wisdom Circles, without which there would be a *lot* fewer stories in this book.

To Riana and Tami who created the GoFundMe so I could have a sabbatical, take my father's ashes to India and take my mother to Scotland as I pursued the very beginnings of this project back in 2019. I still get tears in my eyes thinking about what you did for me.

It takes a village to connect with ancestors and still be cared for in the here and now. Thank you all.

Finally, profound thanks to Bromleigh McCleneghan's editorial magic; not every amazing writer is also an amazing content editor, but she sure is. Also gratitude to David Teems whose copy editing made this such a clean text.